MEDICINE OUTSIDE THE BOX

Musings about health-care issues

PRESCRIPTION
FOR : J.Q. Public
Rx Essays
QTY: 16
S: Take one daily
with a grain of salt
Signature: CamGheat
Repeat: prn

MEDICINE OUTSIDE THE BOX

Musings about health-care issues

Cameron Ghent, M.D.

GSPH

GENERAL STORE PUBLISHING HOUSE
499 O'Brien Road, Box 415
Renfrew, Ontario, Canada K7V 4A6
Telephone 1.613.432.7697 or 1.800.465.6072
www.gsph.com

ISBN 978-1-926962-01-6

Cover art, design, formatting: Magdalene Carson
Printed by Custom Printers of Renfrew Ltd., Renfrew, Ontario
Printed and bound in Canada

Ghent, Cameron
Medicine outside the box : musings on health care issues / Cameron Ghent.
ISBN 978-1-926962-01-6
1. Medical care--Canada. 2. H1N1 influenza--Canada. I. Title.
RA395.C3G54 2011 362.10971 C2011-902980-4

This book is dedicated to the thousands of organ donor family members who, in the midst of personal tragedy and grief, decided to donate organs for transplantation. Because of your generosity and altruism, many of my patients are alive and well, and the transplantation component of my career in medicine has been exciting and fulfilling. You have my sincerest thanks.

Contents

Foreword

When I received the phone call from Dr. Ghent asking if I would write a foreword to his book, I instinctively said "Yes." All the while, I knew that any book written by Cam Ghent would be fascinating and well written, but would contain controversial, if not outrageous, opinions that I would not necessarily share. I was right. It is a fascinating read that demands thought and generates discussion. This is a perfect book for a Book Club—just plan enough time for debate.

Dr. Ghent practised as an academic hepatologist (associate professor), and became Canada's most respected liver transplant physician. Cam worked as a colleague of mine with an office only a few feet from my office at what became referred to in the press as the "Transplant Capital of Canada" in London, Ontario. He was a caring, thoughtful doctor who shunned the limelight and had no social arrogance to him. He was a champion of the patient in virtually all situations but didn't hesitate to voice the blunt, unpleasant facts if they were being ignored for politically correct reasons. He was, in fact, deliberately politically incorrect.

By his own description, he was, and is, an iconoclast. I have had a great fondness and respect for him over the many years but was never spared his criticism when warranted.

With that background, I read this book—*Medicine Outside the Box*.

It is everything I knew it would be. In no particular order, Cam takes the reader on a stroll through his life, commenting on any subject—from the annoying to the absurd, and from the inconvenient to the life-threatening—that he and his patients have had to endure. Not all of the subjects are taken from his area of expertise but they are issues that he has developed opinions on because he has encountered them and then researched them to gain support for his bias. They will undoubtedly provide grist for the mills of those who view the medical profession with suspicion and wish to criticize it. But Cam Ghent can legitimately point out the flaws that need to be addressed because he has practised and researched in one of the most dynamic areas of medicine, contributed to its betterment, and earned the right (and he would say obligation) to critically opine on its shortcomings.

Many of his observations are spot-on and defy explanation as to why they are not corrected. The chapter on Social Distance is an example; very perceptive and lends itself to explain the disparity of opinion that exists on any number of subjects, not the least of which is the view of the adequacy (or inadequacy) of the health-care system.

There is virtually no chapter in this book that will leave the reader without reaction! Whether you agree or not, it will trigger a discussion with a family member or colleague (or even with your doctor!).

Dr. Ghent will undoubtedly be on the media circuit when this book is released, as he is an articulate individual, speaks from experience, and the more controversial opinions in this book will be probed in lively discussions.

I know there's another manuscript cooking in the fertile incubator of Cam Ghent's brain. His ability to point out the absurd borders on a Seinfeld talent, and maybe next time he'll critically observe an area that doesn't hit quite as close to home as this one does! He has a great talent.

For the Canadian reader, Dr. Ghent is to medicine what Rex Murphy is to politics. It doesn't get any better than that!

–Cal Stiller, M.D.

Acknowledgements

Many individuals contributed to this book. The ideas expressed are in part the result of innumerable discussions with colleagues, co-workers, and patients over the course of more than thirty-five years in medical practice. These are too numerous to list individually. I was encouraged by my wife, Vera Simon, my son, Ian, and daughter, Andra, who all reviewed some of the writing for accuracy and flow and made interesting suggestions and revisions. My wife learned to tolerate (and often sleep through) my sudden four a.m. dashes to the home office to get some wording change or new idea down before it left my aging brain. She also suggested the title.

I owe a very special thanks to my tireless, personal copy editor, Lois Hibbert, who took what was often incomprehensible rambling and made it into something that was grammatically correct, readable, and logical. Reginald ("Fish Killer") Gamble suggested that I contact General Store Publishing House, and I am glad that I did. I appreciate the hard work of Senior Editor Jane Karchmar, who encouraged and supported me in whipping the manuscript into a form fit to be published; Magdalene Carson, for her book design; Alison Roesler, publicist; and Tim Gordon, publisher.

Dr. Cal Stiller wrote an apt and perceptive foreword, even though I strongly suspect he disagrees with some of the opinions I express in the book. All of these individuals deserve a lot of credit for their work, but as is always the case, the final responsibility for any remaining errors or inconsistencies is mine and mine alone.

Preface

Cogito, ergo sum.

René Descartes

The possibility of writing a book for the general public about medical issues began to grow slowly in my mind many years ago. In casual discussions with colleagues, co-workers, friends, and patients, I often found that mine was the dissenting opinion and I had trouble agreeing with the conventional wisdom and the standard responses of the medical establishment. But I was concerned that, like a politician abandoning the party line, in sharing these thoughts I would appear to be ungrateful and overly negative about the medical profession and the health-care industry that has served me well. Perhaps my concerns were unfounded; when I realized, as I prepared to retire, that appearances were no longer very important to me, I eventually decided to give it a try.

The actual writing started as I was lying in a hammock on a tropical beach in February 2010, bored because I had run out of interesting reading material on my vacation. When my wife reviewed a first draft of "H1N1" and encouraged me to write more essays, I quickly became a writing fanatic, finding the research and writing therapeutic for myself, if for no one else.

My goal in writing this book is to give the general public a perspective on some of the issues in modern medicine that they may not get from either mainstream media or the medical establishment. As I am now not part of the latter, I saw an opportunity to contribute to the debates that rage daily in both circles. Probably almost every reader, whether in a health-care profession or not, will find something in this book that he will take issue with, and other things with which he will equally strongly agree.

I do not expect everyone to agree with me—that would make for a boring world. I aim to be accurate and to make the reader think "outside the box." If I have succeeded in that, the effort will have been worth it. After all, thinking is what makes us human.

Rx 1

H1N1 — Did We Learn Anything?

Lessons from Darwin and history

The 2009 outbreak of influenza due to a new strain of an old virus presented a serious challenge to public health authorities and to the public. However, the media coverage of this should be remembered as one of the greatest failures in recent medical journalism. On a slow news day, news desk managers could—and did—reliably find some expert to warn us that the worst was yet to come, that this virus selectively kills young, healthy people, and that failure to get vaccinated amounted to irresponsible if not criminal behaviour. Failing that, he or she could find an Alberta pig farmer to fret publicly about the disastrous effects of swine flu on the price of pork belly futures on the Chicago Stock Exchange. In April and May 2009, pigs graced the pages of feature articles in both *Time* magazine and the *Economist*.

We were advised by the media and their obliging experts that this virus could undergo mutation to an even deadlier strain. "Mutation" is a safe term. The word "evolution" might offend creationists who do not acknowledge what they see daily around them as just that—evolution. Mutation is both safer and scarier, and scary headlines sell newspapers. We were given little education about what viruses do as they spread through a community, such as mutating to a less dangerous state. We were not educated at all about the efficacy of the vaccines or the proper ways of evaluating the antiviral treatments used.

Those of us in the business of caring for the sick were required to complete insulting and time-consuming hand hygiene training and to attend a session to be fitted for a tight face mask. To test the mask's effectiveness, individuals unknown to us sprayed malodorous chemicals unknown to us into our faces before and after the fitting. Lacing this spray with some deadly spores would be a terrorist's dream—kill hundreds of health-care workers with no need to commit suicide in the process. Neither a cost analysis nor an assessment of the effectiveness of this process has appeared in either the media or in health publications as far as I can determine.

The missed opportunities to educate the public in this pandemic are legion, but few asked the obvious questions. First, why were young, healthy people apparently selectively afflicted? Very basic biologic principles indicate that the effect of any infection will be more devastating in people with other chronic ailments, if they are equally exposed and equally susceptible. However, in this pandemic, groups were neither equally exposed nor equally susceptible, as many of us oldsters had partial immunity developed from past exposure to related strains of this virus. And, perhaps old folks in nursing homes seldom visit Mexico, the origin of the outbreak in children and youth.

Second, can we be sure that at least some of the fatalities associated with this infection were not associated with a minor mutation in the virus that made it more lethal—both for its host and for itself? That this virus could mutate into an even deadlier strain is true, and it may have happened already, but is hardly a cause for worry. In fact, we might be better off if it did become more lethal to us. The reason for this apparent paradox involves applying the basic evolutionary principle that no organism can increase its spread if, due to the mutation of its individual genes, it increases the death rate of its human host. This is true in all of nature, unless the organism can continue to feed on and spread from the corpse of the host, as in the emerald ash bore beetle infestation of trees, and the bubonic plague in humans in the Middle Ages. In that situation, the corpses and rats in the streets continued to be a source for spread of the invader. But we bury or burn our dead—for just the same reason that we should burn those infected dead ash trees. As Sir Richard Dawkins eloquently argued over thirty years ago,[1] the blind force that impels all organisms to replicate is based in their individual genes. For this analysis, however, the combination of genes that make up a whole organism is the appropriate unit to consider. Apart from the unlucky first few to contact such a superbug, we might, as a species, benefit from a mutation of the H1N1 virus into a more lethal combination of genes that would make it self-destruct.

On the flip side, there are precedents in biology for infectious agents that evolve to cause more benign diseases in their host in order to ensure the organism's own survival. When syphilis ("the French Disease") arrived in Europe in the sixteenth century, it was a deadly disease that was very readily transmitted from disfiguring open skin sores that marked the victim as an undesirable sexual partner. Within fifty years of its arrival, however, it evolved into a more benign disease with the sores largely confined to the genitals, ensuring efficient sexual transmission, while not killing the host.[2] Some epidemiologists are concerned that it may now be hiding itself even more efficiently, with infected individuals developing no symptoms or signs at all. Only the most discriminating philanderer may be able to avoid such an organism.

There is also indisputable evidence that the HIV virus mutates frequently (being a retrovirus, it is "copy error prone," in the scientific jargon) as it reproduces itself. Of these mutations, most probably have little effect on its survival, some will have a negative effect and die out, but others will confer a survival advantage and be selectively propagated. Most of the literature on HIV mutation relates to its ability to become resistant to the various medications used to treat the infection, but limited evidence suggests that the virus may be evolving by natural selection into a less lethal organism. The only concrete evidence that I can find for this is that the frequency of Kaposi's sarcoma, a deadly malignant manifestation of AIDS, as the first symptom or sign of HIV disease, declined dramatically in the first few years of the AIDS epidemic.[3] While the HIV virus makes the job of AIDS researchers difficult by frequently developing drug resistance, it may also be making their job less urgent if it is also developing mechanisms to survive longer in the host without treatment. The implications of this possibility for public health planning are enormous, but it should not reduce the intense effort to develop treatments for this dreadful disease.

The survival instruction manual as it relates to viruses supports giving the host various symptoms—diarrhea, a cough, sneezes, runny nose, or subtle genital sores hidden from any indiscriminate sexual partner but not killing him. The sixth commandment (fifth if you are Roman Catholic), "Thou shalt not kill," applies equally to viruses, bacteria, fungi, and Homo sapiens. This principle explains why human rabies is rare, whereas bat rabies is common. It may also explain why the SARS epidemic died out. SARS was a viral suicide bomber, annihilating itself by its own ferociousness, unable to alter its combination of genes into a more benign and therefore more sustainable form of life. In terms of survival and replication, truly successful viruses such as the common cold, Norwalk virus, and various adenoviruses replicate and spread without killing. The really successful ones such as hepatitis B and HIV integrate themselves into the host's genetic material or, even more effectively, link their fate to the reproductive instincts of the host, ensuring their transmission as we ensure our erotic pleasure and reproduction. Deadly viruses can certainly kill us and still survive and replicate—but only if they do so very slowly over years and have an efficient means of transmission as they are slowly doing us in, as in the case of the human papilloma virus that causes cervical cancer in women.

A third unanswered question relates to treatment effectiveness. In the absence of proper controlled trials, what are we to believe is the real efficacy of the antiviral treatments recommended for established cases? Amid the public panic over this disease in 2009, and without good controlled trials, the United States Food and Drug Administration approved the use of Peramivir, a potent, intravenously administered antiviral that on theoretical grounds should help patients with severe H1N1 infections. We still do not know if it works, because those much-needed controlled trials were pre-empted by the perceived need to give the victims something.

This is a recurring theme in responses to public hysteria about disease outbreaks. A close relative of mine who developed severe SARS in the Toronto 2003 outbreak was given high doses of intravenous ribavarin, a drug that should work to combat SARS. Although it predictably dropped her hemoglobin level dramatically and made her feel awful, whether or not it did anything to improve her chances of survival is impossible to determine, as there were no proper controlled trials of its use in the treatment of SARS.

Dr. Tom Chalmers, one of the pioneers in the development of controlled drug trials in the 1960s and '70s, emphasized the importance of randomizing the first patient when a new treatment is introduced.[4] This is to avoid the development of a bias toward the treatment once the first patient treated improves more than seems likely without the treatment. This apparent effect on the first patient may make it seem unethical to then randomize subsequent sufferers to possibly receive a placebo. The advocates of the new antiviral treatments argue that it is unethical to withhold treatments that have been specifically developed and that should work in life-threatening infections like SARS. I think Dr. Chalmers, if he were still alive, would argue the opposite, that it is unethical to not do the proper controlled trials with randomization of the first patient. Had that been done with ribavarin treatment of SARS, or Peramivir treatment of H1N1 influenza, we would now know whether or not they work. Instead, we may never know. As the sage Pete Seeger asked in 1961, "When will we ever learn?"

Other questions that were never asked, or answered, in the public realm relate to the cost and effectiveness of mass vaccination, compared to other public health priorities, such as smoking cessation programs, or providing other vaccinations. Implementation and promotion of vaccination of preteen girls against that human papilloma virus would allow them to avoid death from cancer of the cervix; perhaps they would live to become old and frail and then die of the flu. The flu "toll" would increase, but so might the number of years the victims lived.

In 2009, the experts and the media encouraged the public to queue up in long lines to get vaccinated. How many of them got infected while waiting with their worried coughing and sneezing neighbours, we will never know. One final question—why were vaccine suppliers to Canada allowed to dictate non-negotiable terms for the sale of the vaccines without accepting any responsibilities for adverse outcomes?

This has been a sad chapter in the annals of medical news coverage. But it is not just the media that failed us in this. The so-called experts who had a chance to do some meaningful public education to better help us understand the dynamics of infections in general also blew it. Perhaps this is in part because they were carefully selected by the media that need sensationalism to get our attention. After all, who is likely to pay any attention to our complicated story about why pathogens tend to evolve to behave more benignly toward us over time when our competition is running with one about a virus that might kill all of us?

Notes

1. Richard Dawkins, *The Selfish Gene* (Oxford: Oxford University Press, 1976).
2. Robert J. Knell, "Syphilis in Renaissance Europe: Rapid Evolution of an Introduced Sexually Transmitted Disease?" *Proc. Biol. Sci.* 271, Suppl. 4 (May 7, 2004): S171–S176.
3. D.C. Des Jarlais, R. Stoneburner, P. Thomas, and S.R. Friedman, "Declines in Proportion of Kaposi's Sarcoma among Cases of AIDS in Multiple Risk Groups in New York City," *Lancet* (October 31, 1987): 1024–25.
4. T.C. Chalmers, "Randomize the First Patient," *New England Journal of Medicine* 107 (1977): 296–97.

Rx 2

Victims

Tainted blood and the victim mentality

If you were seriously injured in an accident prior to 1991, you may well have acquired hepatitis C along with the transfusions used to treat your injuries. That is not your fault, and certainly not fair. None of us that have been blessed with good health and good luck can fully understand the physical and psychological impact of such events. In some limited sense, it does not matter whether you were an at-fault drunk driver, an innocent pedestrian, or injured in some other way; or if you needed transfusions for some blood disorder or a bleeding peptic ulcer. You got a new disease with the treatment, one that you should not have gotten if the blood transfusion services had been taking all the precautions possible to prevent transmission of viruses with the blood products.

In many instances, particularly for those who were transfused prior to 1986, there really was no means to detect hepatitis C contamination of the blood products. The virus was discovered only in 1989, and commercial testing for it became available only in May 1991. Prior to 1986, there was no consensus anywhere in the world that testing for so-called surrogate markers for the virus, such as elevation of blood levels of liver enzymes reflecting liver inflammation in donors, would help to reduce the risk inherent in receiving blood products. It is only with retrospective 20/20 vision that anyone could be said to be at fault for transmission of hepatitis C with blood prior to 1986. That simple fact, however, did not deter the Ontario government from providing politically motivated monetary compensation to those who got hepatitis C from transfusions received prior to 1986 similar to that provided by the federal government for those who got it between 1986 and 1990, although the amounts were lower.

Many people with chronic hepatitis C develop significant, and at times disabling, symptoms after having undiagnosed hepatitis C for years, and these symptoms often become far worse as soon as the diagnosis is made, perhaps in part because they then know that they have a chronic disease. Other individuals deny any symptoms whatsoever and continue to lead normal lives, even with very severe disease. For both groups, symptoms caused by the disease are undoubtedly real, but their severity bears little relationship to the severity of the disease. Experts who study the mechanism of diseases at the cellular and molecular level cannot entirely explain why some people develop symptoms and others do not. We should not expect them to: this mystery cannot be solved without considering the complex psychology involved, including the past experiences and perspectives of the victim.

I have been privileged to interact with and learn from hundreds of hepatitis C victims over twenty years in the course of evaluating and treating their infections. Most feel that someone must be blamed, and that they are owed something. There is plenty of blame to spread around—transfusion services that may not have been as diligent as they should over one time period in screening donors for transmissible infections; doctors who may have ordered transfusions when they were not strictly necessary; and federal regulators of the blood distribution system then in place. However, few of the recipients that I have met have ever expressed any gratitude for the blood donors or the blood services that were available to save their lives, and even fewer seem to understand that they might not even be around to complain if they had not received the blood products.

Another large group of people with chronic hepatitis C infection have taught me a lot. These individuals, who acquired hepatitis C with past intravenous drug use, tattooing, or snorting of street drugs, are victims of their own past poor judgment. As a group, although there are obviously many exceptions, they blame no one but themselves, and once they have coped with their drug abuse issues, they also cope well with having hepatitis C and with its treatment. The psychological concept of locus of control—that is, a person's belief about the amount of control he/she can exert over life events[1]—may be useful here. These folk view themselves as responsible for their past and in control of their future. In contrast, victims of transfusion-acquired hepatitis C have had something terrible done to them, and often sense that control of their lives has been handed over to someone else. Several on-line locus-of-control tests are available and extensively used in psychology to assess personal attributes and attitudes. It would be interesting to see if different victim groups would score differently. On one test that I took, I scored 50/100, but I had the feeling it would really be quite easy to fudge the results. I could respond to the questions to make it look as though I felt helpless—or alternatively to appear as though I felt completely in control of my destiny.

It takes lawyers and politicians to really foul things up, and the "solution" presented for the hepatitis C situation is a prime example. Granted, they acted on pressure from individuals and groups of victims, but they did what lawyers and politicians typically do to redress real or perceived wrongs—they threw other people's money at it. In this case, it was the money of the Canadian taxpayer. For transfusion-acquired hepatitis C, the amount of compensation is determined using a complex system based on the severity of the disease, and on when and where the transfusions were administered. No thought was apparently given to providing these victims any priority access to treatment, either psychological counselling or antiviral treatment to keep their hepatitis C from becoming life-threatening. Jumping the queue for medical treatment is apparently just too un-Canadian to be considered.

I have encountered several victims who refused to take any antiviral treatment to halt the progression of their hepatitis C, confident in the knowledge that if and when the disease progressed, they would be entitled to more monetary compensation, a kind of better-wealthy-than-healthy attitude. Many have requested a liver biopsy, which is often not medically indicated and has some risks, simply because the amount of compensation is based in part on the stage of the disease found on biopsy. When I made the statement at a meeting of the Hepatitis C Society many years ago that paying people to be ill was the worst form of preventative medicine, practised only by lawyers and politicians, I was promptly escorted from the meeting, and asked to not return.

The compensation amounts are not trivial. The 1986–1990 compensation agreement alone has amounted to more than one billion dollars, though how much of that has gone into lawyers' pockets rather than to the victims is apparently not public knowledge. One patient with minimal symptoms and mild hepatitis told me recently that he has received more than $300,000 because he happened to develop an unusual—but easily treated—complication of hepatitis C. The usual range for individual tax-free compensation is from $10,000 just for having the diagnosis, to $240,000 for the estate of someone who died of hepatitis C. There are endless forms to be completed by attending physicians, with no provision for payment directly to them (most of us billed the patients and they included the cost in their claims). We tolerated the transparent hypocrisy of relatives of a long-gone patient asking for a letter, with specific wording dictated by a lawyer, so that they would qualify for the $240,000 in compensation. They usually insisted that they had to go through this process to do justice to the memory of their dearly departed loved one to whom they had perhaps paid little attention while he/she was alive. Presumably $240,000 of taxpayers' money will help them forget the past injustice.

It is not my intent to argue against the need for compassion for those among us who have been wronged or disadvantaged. Our traditional tort law provides a means to rectify such wrongs. The minutiae of legal distinctions between tort law and a system of no-fault societal compensation for bad outcomes rather than for faults have never interested me, and I confess to profound ignorance in legal matters generally. However, it would seem to me that societal compensation for adverse outcomes rather than for fault becomes a very slippery slope. Where does it lead? If we compensate those who acquired hepatitis C with transfusions, while recognizing that no one was at fault, why would we not also compensate someone who has a bad outcome of other interventions, even when no one is at fault? If prostate cancer surgery leads to erectile dysfunction, no one is at fault, as that is a recognized and unavoidable consequence of such surgery in some men. Should we then compensate all those men from the public purse, or at least pay for their Viagra?

Overcoming the victim mentality is obviously not easy, and I have no magic formula to do so. In one sense, it does not matter if the damage is done by a hurricane, a blood transfusion, or our own vanity, as in the case of the harm allegedly caused by some silicone breast implants. Liberal television news programs that daily find new victims to report on may increase our sense of sympathy and our generosity. However, they also reinforce the public's expectations that life should be fair, one of the surest means of making everyone disappointed and angry. Pop psychology programs that provide trite advice about getting over it and getting on with life seldom seem to help either, but at least do little harm, and may be closer to the right direction. Somehow the best outcomes can be expected with a convergence of medical, psychological, and sociological studies. My hunch is that restoring the vague concept of locus of control to within the person is somehow a key to this process. Money certainly is not.

A remarkable statement by the remarkable widow of a police officer who was shot in our area in March 2010 stands out as a wonderful example of insight into getting over the victim mentality very quickly. At his funeral, she is reported to have said, "As hard as it is, I believe forgiveness is the only way to release us from the pain and anger." This profound insight made me wonder if she was influenced by some contact with our First Nations peoples. These people were derisively labelled as noble savages by the savage nobles of our advanced judiciary, with their wigs and robes disguising their mendacity. However, the Native elders consider concepts of forgiveness and restoration of community as well as punishment, when one of their own has committed some crime and appears before a sentencing circle. In contrast, in our so-called advanced justice system, with victim impact statements in court and class action suits, the concentration is on money and punishment, appealing to our baser instincts for revenge. Who is more savage and who is more noble in this comparison?

In spite of these negative comments about victims, if an inept surgeon were to lop the wrong appendage off this aging body, I suspect that I would immediately assume the victim role and seek out the best litigation lawyer I could find. I am sure I could not forgive as quickly as that widow did.

Notes

1. For an excellent but dated review of the Locus of Control construct, see Herbert M. Lefcourt, *Locus of Control: Current Trends in Research and Practice* (New York: Lawrence Erlbaum Associates, 1982).

℞ 3

PSA

The sick prostate cancer industry

A relative of mine was diagnosed with prostate carcinoma at the age of fifty-eight. This was not because of symptoms or on the basis of abnormal physical examination findings, but because he was persuaded to have a routine screening blood test called the prostate-specific antigen (PSA) test. Since the result was slightly high, he had a biopsy of his prostate that proved he had cancer. On a urologist's recommendation, he underwent surgical removal of his prostate gland, with serial measurement of the blood PSA level thereafter. More than a year later, when the PSA level began to rise from zero, after more scans and blood tests, radiation to the site where the prostate gland had been was recommended, and he travelled daily five days a week for six weeks to a cancer centre sixty kilometres from his home for the treatments. A couple of years later, when the blood PSA level rose again, he had more x-rays and scans, and then started on chemotherapy with an antagonist to testosterone, as it is known that prostate cancer growth is promoted by testosterone. When the PSA level rose even more on this therapy, the experts recommended further experimental chemotherapy for him, supervised at a site eighty kilometres from his home.

Who has benefited from this sequence of events? The urologists, radiation therapists, oncologists, radiologists, laboratory technicians, and medical/pharmaceutical industry have all benefited in the above scenario, largely at the expense of the taxpayer in a publicly funded system. But has the patient?

Cancer of the prostate is very common and not to be taken lightly. However, it is also usually a very slow-growing tumour that often stays confined to the prostate gland for years after it develops and may never spread or become life threatening. It is estimated that about 30 percent of men over the age of sixty and 50 percent of those over seventy have prostate cancer. It should not be viewed in the same way as many other treatable diseases that can be cured only if found early with routine screening. The public perspective and media attention with the presumption that early detection and treatment of disease is always beneficial simply does not apply to this cancer.

It is probably not realistic to expect the average layperson to ignore the advice to be screened for treatable disease, especially when the disease has the emotional baggage of the word "cancer." Furthermore, he is not likely to get advice to ignore screening from medical experts whose livelihood depends on treating the diseases they find. It would take a very unusual and brave urologist to give the career-limiting advice to any man referred for treatment of prostate cancer to just live with it.

The old-fashioned and undignified rectal examination screening test for prostate carcinoma has given way to more sophisticated screening tests, such as variations on the blood PSA test and various ways of imaging the gland. Since almost none of the studies of treatment outcome have reported separately on groups of men whose tumours were found or at least suspected with rectal examination alone compared with other tests, we cannot accurately determine the incremental advantage of the more sophisticated tests. One Scandinavian study[1] reported that at twelve years after diagnosis, the chances of being disease free was increased by treatment in only one out of twenty men who had been treated, and 75 percent of the patients in that study had had their tumour detected with the simplest test–a rectal examination. This means that at least nineteen out of twenty men who have undergone treatment for prostate cancer have been shown to have not benefited twelve years later, and have probably endured some of the negative effects of the diagnosis and treatment that my relative has. It is estimated from that study that between fifty and 200 men need to be treated to ultimately prevent one death from prostate cancer. Most men over the age of seventy will die with prostate cancer, but not of it, and PSA testing does a poor job of making the distinction between serious life-limiting prostate cancer and the more common slow-growing kind that will never do you in. No test to date has proven very effective in making this distinction.

My relative has lived for more than eight years with the knowledge that he has cancer and for six of those years with the knowledge that it is not curable. Until recently, he had no symptoms except for those related to the treatments. He has had costly and inconvenient blood tests, scans, radiation, and chemotherapy, with trips to the cancer clinic to remind him of his plight, and constant anxiety about his future. The conversation at family gatherings often turns to his latest PSA level. The evidence that any of what he has experienced has altered his funeral date is skimpy at best. If the biopsy that was done before the prostate was removed had by chance moved some malignant cells from within the gland to along the path of the needle used for the biopsy, a harmless cancer might have been converted into an incurable one by the test used to determine how severe it was. "Needle tract seeding" is a well-documented risk of placing a needle in any malignant tissue, whether in the liver, breast, thyroid gland, or prostate.

By now, those of my colleagues and friends who have had treatment for prostate cancer and who have read this far may be secretly hoping that I will develop a rapidly progressive form of this disease in retribution for seemingly questioning their judgment in having this therapy. I do not question their judgment—there is no easy answer, and each individual has to make tough decisions when faced with this disease or the prospects of having it, and individual circumstances vary tremendously. Nor is it my intention to question the integrity of the professionals who do their best in treating this disease. On the contrary, I hope these brave patients have provided their doctors with enough experience with this problem that by the time I need the treatment it will have been refined to perfection.

It is my intent, however, to point out that there is another side to this dilemma. I am not the best expert to consult for advice about caring for your prostate, but neither are a host of celebrities who have had treatment for prostate cancer, including Arnold Palmer, Bob Dole, Colin Powell, Rudy Giuliani, Harry Belafonte, John Kerry, and Jack Layton, most of whom have become vociferous advocates for routine screening with the PSA test. It is not possible with the information available in the public domain to determine whether any of these individuals would not have been around to do the advocating on behalf of the prostate cancer industry if they had not been screened, but the odds are good that all of them would be. We do know that in the case of John Kerry, his prostate cancer was diagnosed by detecting a rise in PSA levels over a few months, all of those levels being within the normal range, as his doctor has crowed about the wonderful feat of making the diagnosis before the levels became abnormal. The logical extension of this thinking is to recommend that every man over the age of sixty (John Kerry's age at diagnosis) should have the PSA test every few months. Or does this apply only if your patient is a prominent politician? We do know that politicians and other public figures are at high risk for getting poor medical care and advice (see Chapter 7). We also know that, contrary to popular reports, Bob Dole's father died with prostate cancer, but not of it.

The psychological phenomenon known as the endowment effect,[2] also known as the divestiture aversion effect or ownership bias, makes it hard to acknowledge that you may have made a mistake or done something that did not need to be done. Like buying a new car that turns out to be a lemon, it may be hard to acknowledge that it really is a lemon. Once "endowed" with treatment for prostate cancer, it is very difficult for such individuals to be unbiased. This is particularly difficult if you sit on the board of a company with investments in the research and treatment of prostate cancer, and you become a paid spokesman for the treatment of the erectile dysfunction that commonly results from the treatment, as in the case of Bob Dole. "Battling cancer," as the media invariably portray these individuals, is hardly a heroic endeavour if it is a fight you did not need to pick in the first place. But how can you tell?

What is my own approach? I hesitantly declined my family physician's offer to order a PSA test after she assured me that my prostate felt completely normal, only to have the test done anyway a few months later, made necessary by an insurance company apparently looking for any excuse to decline my application for a change in my life insurance.

Everyone needs to make an informed decision in this difficult area. To simply avoid making one is not good enough. Every man should discuss this with his doctor, and not blindly accept the standard recommendations. Quiz your doctor closely—what has he done for his own prostate? Or if you have a female doctor, what has she advised her male partner to do about his prostate? For those who are more proactive in health matters, get involved in advocacy for balanced educational programs, and in studies that properly evaluate means of preventing, detecting, and treating this disease. Reflexive responses to the word "cancer" should not be applied to this one.

Notes

1. F.H. Schroder, J. Hugosson, M.J. Roobol, T.L.J. Tammela, et al., "Screening and Prostate-Cancer Mortality in a Randomized European Study," *New England Journal of Medicine* 360 (2009): 1320–28.
2. The endowment effect is extensively discussed by Richard T. Thaler and Cass R. Sunstein in their book, *Nudge: Improving Decisions about Health, Wealth, and Happiness* (London, UK: Penguin Books, 2008).

Rx 4

Prescriptions

Drug wars: Rx version 1.0

Why, in Canada currently, are some dangerous drugs available without a prescription, while others that are very safe and effective are either available by prescription only or not available at all? Why are some very effective drugs withdrawn inexplicably and replaced with other less effective ones? Why are some drugs available in the United States but not in Canada? The following four examples illustrate these situations.

The most common cause of fatal acute liver failure in North America is accidental, or at times deliberate, overdosing on a non-prescription drug called acetaminophen. It is available in at least a dozen different preparations from multiple manufacturers and with different trade names, and is advertised as effective for arthritis, colds and flu, and headaches. It is an effective painkiller and is often combined with other ingredients such as small doses of codeine and caffeine. Because it is available over the counter in multiple preparations with different names, it is easy to mistakenly take too much—one pill for your arthritis, another for your fever, and a third for your flu headache, all with different names—and you may end up in coma in an intensive care unit with a failing liver. It has a narrower therapeutic window (the difference between an effective therapeutic dose and a toxic one) than many drugs that are available only by prescription and that come with a "black box warning" about potentially serious toxicity. Even the oral form of marijuana, pure tetrahydrocannabinol or THC, is safer than acetaminophen but can be obtained only by written prescription with a carefully worded specific format, as it is categorized as a narcotic, like morphine or heroin. Combine acetaminophen with an alcoholic beverage, another drug with serious toxicity ("spirits fermenti" in older prescriptions for bedtime whisky), and the dose needed to damage your liver is even lower. So why is it available without a prescription?

Neomycin is a safe oral antibiotic that was used to treat confusion and coma associated with severe liver diseases of all kinds until it was withdrawn from the market by the manufacturer in 2000, without explanation either to practitioners or apparently to the Food and Drug Directorate. It is still available as a topical agent for skin and ear infections and for veterinary use. Your veterinarian can prescribe it, but your physician cannot. The alternative drug to use for liver disease in humans, Rifaxamin, is licensed for use in the United States but not in Canada. So why was neomycin withdrawn from the market and why was the alternative never approved for use in Canada?

Trientene is what is called an orphan drug (a drug that has only one indication, and that for a rare situation) that is very effective in the treatment of a rare genetic disease called Wilson disease. Experts in this disease generally believe that trientene is as effective as and safer than the standard approved treatment drug called D-penicillamine. The guidelines for treatment of Wilson disease, however, continue to advocate use of D-penicillamine for first-line treatment, largely because of difficulties in getting trientene for these patients. The Canadian marketing rights for trientene have undergone a series of changes and it has never been approved by Health Canada for use, but can be obtained on a compassionate basis for certain patients *if* the patient provides his or her confidential medical information to the president of the Wilson Disease Society in the United States *and* the prescribing physician is willing to fill out an inordinate amount of paperwork for the patient. So why did this bizarre situation develop?

Triampterine was an effective diuretic for treatment of excess fluid accumulation in people with cirrhosis from any cause. It was inexplicably withdrawn from the market in 2002. That left physicians with the choice of prescribing aldactone or a weaker diuretic called amiloride to balance out the effects of so-called potassium-wasting diuretics such as furosemide, on patients' serum potassium levels. But ameloride often fails to control the fluid accumulation, which leaves aldactone as the only alternative.

Unfortunately, aldactone produces painful and sometimes striking breast enlargement in a high proportion of men using it (no such enlargement occurs in women—sorry, ladies). Men needing to use a potassium-sparing diuretic now often have no choice but to use aldactone and put up with the whistles in the locker room. Where were their concerns addressed when the decision was made to stop the manufacture of triampterene?

These four examples of problems with use of medication have been drawn from the narrow field of hepatology (the study of liver disease) and raise broader issues concerning the regulation of drug use and drug availability in Canada. I am sure each specialty has similar problems and examples within its field.

The relationship of the prescribing physician and the dispensing pharmacist has a long and noble history and uses a Latin-based language sure to mystify the patient. This relationship is now being challenged by granting nurse practitioners the right to prescribe certain medications and by allowing pharmacists in certain jurisdictions to dispense some prescription-only medications without a physician's prescription. But the arguments about who should or should not be able to prescribe and/or fill prescriptions overshadow several much bigger questions that are seldom asked. One question that needs the joint attention of physicians, pharmacists, and regulatory bodies is how to determine whether a drug, new or old, should be available: through the Internet, over the counter, by prescription only, or not at all. A second is what factors determine that a drug should be available by prescription only.

The current system is bogged down in historical precedents and, one suspects, a lot of lobbying and deference to the pharmaceutical development industry, and the retail pharmacy industry. Try, for example, to compare a pharmacist's profit margin for a given drug sold over the counter as opposed to by prescription and one encounters a brick wall. Historical precedents are not good enough in making these decisions. Historical precedents are the reason we have dangerous drugs such as aspirin available over the counter, and why we do not have some valuable and safe drugs available at all.

In dealing with large pharmaceutical companies and their drug development programs over many years, I can appreciate the profit motive in drug development. A company that has spent hundreds of millions of dollars to develop a new drug should expect a fair market price to recover its investment, but the need for a prescription to obtain a drug should have nothing to do with making a profit or with the dispensing cost to the pharmacist. One cannot escape the suspicion that both parties have profit in mind when applying for a licence to market a new drug as a prescription-only agent. Once a particular product has lost its profitability, as seems to be the case with neomycin, cited earlier, it should not simply be allowed to be pulled from the shelves because the patent has elapsed or because the market is too small. There should also be some convenient means of accommodating the needs of small numbers of patients who need a drug such as trientene, which is not approved at all, apparently because the costs of going through the approval process would exceed any revenue from sales. Who is considering the needs of the patients in this process?

The assertion that the decisions about which drugs should be available by prescription only is based on protecting the public from dangerous doses of dangerous drugs is patently false. If that were the case, acetaminophen would be available in only one formulation, by prescription only, and probably with a black box warning about its serious toxicity. Aspirin might well be categorized as a totally illegal drug for sale in Canada if it were discovered today—it would certainly not be available without a prescription. On a theoretical basis, if aspirin and acetaminophen were both restricted to prescription use, it seems likely that someone would by now have discovered and marketed safer alternative analgesics that would not need a prescription. If safety was the basis for deciding whether or not you need a prescription from a physician, nurse, or pharmacist, many new drugs would never need a prescription. The worst possible outcome of, for example, a massive overdose of lactulose, a drug available only by prescription, is that your colon would be well prepared for a thorough colonoscopy. Why do the very safe proton-pump inhibitors used to suppress stomach acid secretion require a prescription, whereas the histamine receptor blockers that do the same thing are available over the counter?

Many new drugs are safer than alcohol, a dangerous drug that is available without a prescription, although not from a pharmacist. Why was quinine sulfate, a very safe and effective agent for nocturnal leg cramps available without a prescription a few years ago, moved to now requiring one? This example is doubly confusing, since one can get the equivalent dose of quinine from a couple cans of tonic water, without the gin.

There are good theoretical reasons for limiting antibiotics to prescription status. The main one is the fear that indiscriminate use will lead to a worsening problem, with bacteria developing resistance. However, like most beliefs held with religious fervour, this one has apparently not been rigorously tested. In many countries, over-the-counter antibiotics are readily available. Do they have more problems with multi-drug resistant bacteria than we do? I cannot find any answer to that question. There are limited circumstances where logic would indicate that some antibiotics might be appropriately used and made available without a prescription in Canada. If you develop a painful abscessed tooth on a Saturday night, why should you need to spend several hours in a busy emergency room waiting to be seen by a grouchy dentist, when the forgone conclusion is that you will be given a prescription for a penicillin derivative? Could the pharmacist not have confirmed the diagnosis and dispensed this without the delay and inconvenience of an emergency room visit? Even more convincing is the situation with respect to minor venereal infections such as chlamydia, when the treatment should include the sexual partner(s) of the patient, many of whom will refuse to be tested or treated if they need to visit a doctor and get a prescription. The British in fact have made azithromycin available without a prescription for physician-confirmed cases of chlamydia infection in women, but not for their partners. How stupid is that? Without making the treatment available to the partners as well, this will not do much to reduce the transmission of this infection.

The argument that the need for a prescription is in part related to the need for precise instructions for proper use and effectiveness of a drug also does not bear up to close scrutiny. In the Internet age, information on how to use a drug appropriately can be dispensed on paper or by referring patients to a reliable Internet address, with or without a prescription. Apart from the implicit paternalism of a physician and/or pharmacist always being needed to instruct you in how to take a drug appropriately, one could legitimately question whether their time could not be more appropriately utilized if they used the Internet for routine instructions and concentrated on instructing people on the proper use of really dangerous drugs like chemotherapeutic agents and acetaminophen, or interactions of several drugs.

Delve into the world of pharmaceutical regulation on the Internet to find answers to what is really considered in determining the prescription status of either new or old drugs in Canada, and one sinks quickly into a quagmire of opaque red tape, associations, bureaus, advisory boards, directorates, departments, and different levels of government that will leave you gasping for air. The word "prescription" cannot be found in most of these sites, so it must be assumed within the National Association of Pharmacy Regulatory Authorities that all newly marketed drugs require a prescription. The striking impression in scanning these sites is the detail that is gone into on the evaluation and monitoring of applications for new drugs, and the lack of any concern with regulation of old prescription or non-prescription drugs. But what about these older drugs? Particularly the non-prescription drugs, the ones the manufacturers decide to no longer market for financial reasons, or those whose market is too small to justify the cost of going through an application for licensing? The problems associated with *not* looking into these are as important as those associated with licensing new ones.

With multiple formularies, agencies, and departments of different levels of governments, it is easy to understand why no one group of nameless bureaucrats has gone to the trouble of looking at the big picture and the historical precedents to consider the rational basis for the need of a prescription. To do so would inevitably lead to jurisdictional squabbles between the various regulatory bodies and governments, and between departments in the same level of government. To not do so is to leave the best interests of the patient in the hands of those who have many reasons to tinker with the status quo without meaningful change. The patients lose out.

It is not time to completely throw away the prescription pad, as some radicals on both the left and the right would propose, for different reasons. But it *is* time to take a careful look at what the need for a prescription means. With Canadians now spending more annually on prescription drugs than on physicians' services, we should be asking some tough questions about the whole business of prescriptions, not just about who writes them. There needs to be some consensus developed among all health-care professionals, with input from unbiased economists as to which medications require a prescription and which do not. Leaving this to the vested interests of physicians, pharmacists, and the impotent bureaucrats of Ottawa will not reduce costs nor improve the safety of medication use.

Rx 5

Money and Motives

Doctoring the doctor business for profit

One of the major differences between the Canadian and the American systems of health care is the financial aspect of who pays for what. Americans are dedicated to making a profit in every enterprise, whereas in Canada, for-profit medical care is a political hot potato. This difference persists in spite of the recent legislated changes in American health care. We are so indoctrinated in the myth that health care is and should be free to all, that if someone is seen to be making a profit from the care of patients, other than by billing the provincial insurance plan, we have politicians screaming about a two-tiered system and the destruction of the universal health-care system that defines who we are.

However, some basic logic would indicate that we already have something far less than universal health care and something that strongly resembles a two-tier for-profit system. My teeth and my eyesight are important to my health, and the care of them is not, with some exceptions, covered by the provincial "universal" health-care plan. Nor is the cost of prescription drugs that may be as important to my health as the visits to the doctor. This is two-tier care in that only those who have a dental plan, an eye care plan, or a prescription drug plan through their employer have "free" access to these services—but even if your employer provides these plans at no out-of-pocket cost to you, they will inevitably impact your take-home pay, as the expense is a cost of doing business. Furthermore, the outlay for these from your benefits plan will be treated at least in part as taxable income by the same politicians who rave about the free universal Canadian health-care system.

Why is the practice of medicine viewed differently than

other professions when it comes to making money in this country? If your divorce attorney suggests that you take the proposed settlement agreement to court, rather than settling, you may well question the motivation—is she acting in your best interests or merely prolonging the agony at your expense for her benefit? If your dentist recommends expensive root canal work you may well ask the same question. If the veterinarian recommends expensive blood tests on your ailing antique cat, you may question whether the expense is worth it. However, if your family physician recommends that you have a set of routine blood rests as part of your annual checkup, you are likely to accept the recommendation without questioning the motives.

The profit motive is seldom questioned in the alternative medicine and herbal remedy fields, but is at least as operative as in mainstream medical practice. No brass bracelet for your arthritis is likely to be sold to you at a loss; the same applies to naturopathic cleanses practitioners will sell to you to purify your liver. You expect them to make a profit with these products. But there is a subtle difference when it comes to expecting your doctor to make a profit. It is also seen as somehow improper to question what the physician may make in providing a given service. It should not be. Why the difference?

Part of the answer lies in differing levels of trust we place in these different professionals. However, part also relates to the fact that you are likely to see, and pay for out of your pocket, the bills submitted by the attorney, dentist, veterinarian, and health store producer but not that of your physician. For minor items such as routine blood tests, it is unlikely that the physician even knows how much the tests cost. However, that is not the case for a vast array of visits, and other tests and procedures your family physician or specialist recommends. If the gastroenterologist or surgeon recommends a routine upper gastrointestinal endoscopy or a colonoscopy, a different set of dynamics is set in motion—he is likely to do the procedure and to bill the insurance plan, whether public or private, for its cost, at the rate the Schedule of Benefits or other remuneration system allows. There is then a question of monetary motivation, the same question that is much more likely to be asked about the attorney, dentist, veterinarian, or naturopath.

Graduating medical students often have accumulated significant debts during the course of their training. A high priority for most of them, and a reasonable one, is to get rid of that debt. They must choose an area of practice, whether as a family physician or in some other specialty. Most of them are very cognizant of the realities that some specialties have the potential to generate far more income than others. They would not be human to ignore this factor completely. Apart from issues related to lifestyle (dermatologists are seldom seen on hospital wards at three a.m.), this discrepancy must play some part in the decision to choose one specialty over another. It is no coincidence that the most popular specialties happen to be those that have the highest earning potential. But not all graduates can train to become dermatologists, radiologists, ophthalmologists, or plastic surgeons; only a limited number of training positions are allotted to each specialty. Applicants rank their selection of training programs nationally, and the non-profit Canadian Resident Matching Service (CaRMS) then supervises and administers the matching of applicant trainees to programs in an annual mating ritual as complicated as that of many birds. It is a stressful and intense process that gives graduates and programs alike an incentive to at least present a rosy picture of themselves to the suitor.

CaRMS does not see as its primary mandate any assurance that the number of people trained in each specialty matches the number needed to provide care to the population at large, nor does any one single regulatory body. Fortunately, provincial and federal bodies such as the Royal College of Physicians and Surgeons of Canada exercise some control of the selection process. The Royal College basically arbitrarily determines the number of training positions available at each tertiary care centre for each specialty, by accreditation of the training programs. However, this process often conflicts with the goals of training programs to recruit the brightest and best graduates—trainees do a lot of the humdrum work within teaching hospitals, and provide a good academic environment for faculty, as well as opportunities and manpower for research with the teachers in an academic division or department. The training programs' goals may have nothing to do with the real needs of the population, present or future.

The question that must be asked is: Does this matching process and the number of people trained in each specialty reflect the needs of the current or projected future population? The job of CaRMS is to fill the training slots available at each academic centre with the least dissatisfaction of the trainees and the training program faculty. Where a graduate ends up getting training and in what specialty is largely determined by the ranking they give to various programs, and how the program directors rank the applicants. Someone who desperately wants to become a rheumatologist in New Brunswick may end up training as a psychiatrist or hematologist in Edmonton, although such extreme mismatching is fortunately rare.

Current practising family physicians are in a better position than almost anyone else to know what specialties are most needed; they are the ones who must plead and cajole and spend endless hours on the phone trying to get their patients seen by a specialist in a timely fashion. They are also almost completely excluded from the process of deciding how many graduates of each specialty the system produces each year.

It is clear that in an economic system where the market demand for medical care is fluid and apparently unlimited, the laws of supply and demand simply do not work. What is available—the supply—is to a large degree what training programs produce; and what is needed—the demand—adjusts to what is available, rather than to the actual needs for care. For example, we supplied many excellent surgeons in the very demanding skills of liver transplantation (see Chapter 6) only to find that there were no places for them to perform this procedure once they had finished their training. Most returned to the more mundane but more profitable practice of general surgery. We currently have well-trained gastroenterologists whose training is largely wasted when they discover that they cannot find a hospital with available procedure time in which to practise the skills they have learned.

A new practitioner has ample opportunity within a fee-for-service system to maximize the chances of paying off the student loans quickly. Some such income-maximizing strategies simply annoy patients and generate ill-will, such as billing the patient for telephone renewals of prescriptions for drugs that should not require a prescription anyway (see Chapter 4) or for missed appointments. The family physician who insists that you make three separate appointments to assess your hypertension, your diabetes, and your rash is using the system for financial reward, but so is the insurance plan bureaucrat who expects the physician to address all three problems for one minor assessment fee. Such strategies, however, do not compromise the quality of patient care.

Other routines motivated by income considerations may be less visible to patients. In my practice, standard routine required patients to return a couple of weeks after a liver biopsy or endoscopy for discussion of the results, even though I may well have been able to do this on the phone or through a letter to the referring physician—but the rules of the game are that phone calls and letter-writing are freebies. I could bill the insurer only for a face-to-face visit. I was able to persuade myself that this practice was necessary after hearing many patients complain that they never did get feedback after having a procedure done by others, but I was also cognizant of the monetary implications. This need for face-to-face contact may well also partially explain why telehealth services have not reached their full potential. With a good audiovisual link, I could probably do a very adequate consultation on a patient 1,000 miles away, but the fee schedule would not allow me to bill for that service. The same arcane rules of billing also indicate that I could have done much better financially if I could have persuaded each referring physician to send a three-word letter with every one of the chronic liver disease patients I reviewed once a year—"Please review annually." I could then bill a consultation fee with each annual visit, rather than the lesser amount for a limited assessment.

Still other strategies to increase income that are not obvious to the patient may well impact the quality of care. Some gastroenterologists spend three days a week doing upper gastrointestinal endoscopies or colonoscopies with an almost 1:1 ratio of patients seen to patients having procedures done, while other specialists in the same field see four patients for every one they deem to have an indication for a procedure. The latter spend a lot more time solving the problem with a detailed history and physical examination and selective laboratory testing along with some head-scratching. Obviously, the indications for procedures are flexible enough to fit in the number of patients that such a specialist has procedure time for, should he choose that option. The same variability seems to apply to surgical specialties. The indications for operations cannot be easily separated from the availability of operating room time. It is easy for the surgeon to decide that you do not really need to have your gallbladder removed if she has no operating room time to do that; it is equally easy to decide that your gallbladder should be removed if there happens to be a cancellation leading to available operating room time next Friday. Procedure time and operating room time within hospitals is prized and fiercely protected by those who have been granted it, not because all of the patients need procedures, but because your doctor can probably make at least twice the amount of money in the hospital doing procedures as he can in the equivalent amount of time doing consultations in the outpatient clinic or office.

Most patients are only vaguely, if at all, aware of these subtle ways their physician may be maximizing income, or the impact this may have on their care. An older teacher at an academic centre taught me, only half in jest, that there were four broad general categories of indications for endoscopic examinations—diagnostic, therapeutic, punitive, and remunerative. At times he was able to combine these indications, by, for example, punitive endoscopy to prove to you that your irritable bowel symptoms were not serious and you should stop complaining about them, and at the same time confirm the diagnosis and collect a hefty remuneration. Many people with a severe bellyache no longer own an appendix because they had an "acute remunerative appendicitis." Primary care physicians provide monthly injections of vitamin B12 (read office visit fee) to many more people than actually have pernicious anemia—fortunately, B12 injections may also be legitimately used as a safe placebo for the worried well person.

As the examples above indicate, current fee schedules provide a powerful incentive for practitioners in all areas to tailor their practice routines to maximize income. Even so, most physicians do not bill insurers all that they could for services actually provided. In the midst of a busy practice, it takes a real dedication to monetary gain to study the complex Schedule of Benefits in sufficient detail to bill for everything that would be allowed. Most would prefer to forego a few dollars rather than risk triggering an audit of their billing by the insurer, or worse still, having their name appear in the *Toronto Star* as an example of a greedy doctor who overbilled the taxpayer.

It is interesting to note what is and is not allowed in the Schedule of Benefits in various jurisdictions and how new services such as endoscopic ultrasound assessments get into the remuneration schedule. Part of this process is to review what experts recommend as standard care. I have served on a few practice guideline development committees to make recommendations to practitioners and noted the great care taken to exclude any influence by industry, particularly drug manufacturers. The committees are less careful in assessing what effect the guidelines may have in generating income for the specialists involved in developing the guidelines. It is unlikely that the guidelines for prostate cancer screening (see Chapter 3) published by the American Urological Society were developed by individuals with no interest in ever doing prostate surgery for a living. The guideline indications made by gastroenterologists for colon cancer screening would no doubt change quickly if the fees for colonoscopy were drastically reduced. The same can be said for the recommendations for the same screening process made by radiologists if the fees for virtual colonoscopy or barium enema examinations were altered. A third iteration of the recommendations would be made if regulations were ever altered to allow specially trained nurses to do colonoscopies.

There is nothing intrinsically wrong with doctors being motivated in part to make money in the practice of medicine. However, there is a danger that without some checks and balances, the profit motive can lead to inappropriate over-servicing of a general public that is not very sophisticated about what is and what is not necessary medical care and that tends to equate more health-care service with better service. The hospital with two magnetic resonance imaging machines and a positron emission scanning service must be able to provide better care than one that only has computed tomography capacity, right? The advertisement that Centre X can do complete head-to-toe imaging and provide a printout of your coronary artery calcification score and the thickness of the cholesterol plaque in your carotid artery is appealing to the worried well who are always concerned that a stroke or heart attack is just around the corner and that only this type of preventative searching is going to find and prevent the problem. But is Centre X offering this service for altruistic reasons to help you keep healthy? Or does the fact that such services generate a substantial profit enter into its decision to offer the service? In the United States, such centres are commonly said to accept anyone who is fiscally fit.

With some very limited exceptions—examples would include mammography for women over age fifty, cervical cancer screening in women, annual prostate examinations for men over fifty or sixty, and just possibly routine testing and treatment of elevated cholesterol levels in healthy adults—the evidence that searching for and treatment of any disease in symptom-free adults is helpful to the patient is dubious at best, but it is certainly helpful for the provider's pocketbook. Even the evidence that you will benefit from having your cholesterol level checked, let alone treated, is questionable unless you have other risk factors for vascular disease. What this testing does do is give the laboratory some taxpayer-paid business and the physician a reason to bill for more office visits. It also gives the pharmaceutical industry a handsome income. In Canada, annual sales of serum cholesterol-lowering agents is on the order of $1 billion, with considerable debate about who is benefiting the most from this, the patient, the doctor, the pharmacist, the laboratories that do the testing, or the pharmaceutical manufacturers.

Governments, i.e., insurers for health care, are rightly also motivated by monetary considerations as they struggle to use taxpayers' money responsibly. Government health-care planners are well aware of the potential for providing more services than necessary in order to profit in a fee-for-service system where there is no disincentive to provide services that are unnecessary and may even be harmful. Interestingly, experiments to increase patients' awareness of the costs of services by providing a printout of the services billed to the health plan for each physician encounter have generally backfired on the bureaucrats—when the patients see the bill, they generally feel that the doctor's pay has been inadequate.

Economist Steven Levitt[1] has written extensively about motivating people to do the right thing and the consequences of that motivation. Money is a powerful motivator, whether, as he has documented, in the perpetuation of the oldest profession, or in the decision of the new medical graduate to train in a high-income specialty to more quickly pay off student loans. If we found an equally powerful motivator to persuade graduates to select a specialty that would be more beneficial to the public they care for, we might all be better off. But how do we do that?

Several alternatives to fee-for-service, including capitation, a flat salary, and a fee-for-service plan with a cap, are being tested in different settings. Having worked for many years with trainees who are on a flat salary system and do not participate in fee-for-service billing, I am concerned that that system creates a disincentive to provide service. Arguments abound in teaching hospitals about who is responsible for what. If you are eighty-five, with multiple medical problems, and show up with shortness of breath in the emergency room of a teaching hospital, it is likely that the residents will try hard to pass your care off to whoever is least able to say no. They will spend an inordinate amount of time reading through your chart to see if someone who saw you previously might be prevailed upon to do the admitting history and physical examination and assume responsibility for your ongoing care. You will not be made to feel welcome and needed in the same way that you would if each of your chronic problems was being assessed and cared for by a practitioner being paid on a fee-for-service basis.

A recent study by British psychologist Christopher Boyce[2] clearly shows that money does not buy happiness, but there is evidence that making more of it than your peers is a source of happiness, at least for most Brits. Those who were wealthy in this study but were not better off than their peers were no happier than the poor. This suggests that eliminating the fee-based discrepancies in doctors' incomes would just leave everyone unhappy. This finding has enormous implications for health-care economists. There seems, on the basis of this study, to be no reason to think that an equalization of income for all specialties whether with a flat salary system or with correcting the gross inequities in the Schedule of Benefits in a fee-for-service system, would be effective in balancing the needs of the professionals with the needs of the public, and it might, in fact, harm the process.

Addressing inequities in remuneration is nevertheless important in attracting trainees to much-needed specialties, but the societies of high-paying specialties fiercely protect the status quo—witness the lawsuit launched by the Ontario Association of Radiologists against the Ontario Medical Association a few years ago. It is easier to increase the fees of low-income specialties than to decrease those of the more lucrative, but with a limited budget, that is not able to narrow the gap much. The family physicians and their organizations also need to have more input into the decisions about the number of trainees being produced—for their own specialty and for others. Some drastic changes to what is covered in the Schedule of Benefits are also needed, e.g., accepting that a detailed telehealth consultation or a long letter of explanation to a patient is as worthy of remuneration as is a face-to-face encounter.

What may also help is finding some motivator other than money to give practitioners more satisfaction with their work. Perhaps they could benefit more from a sense that they are making a real difference in the lives of their patients, rather than just making money. This takes us all the way back to picking out students applying for medical school and examining their motives to do so. We have never been very good at that. In ancient times, when I was asked at the admissions committee meeting on application to medical school why I wanted to be a doctor, I naively but honestly replied that I admired my family doctor, and wanted to be like him. In reality, it was his daughter, my high school classmate and academic competitor, whom I was fond of.

Could we not now use a battery of sophisticated psychological tests and a structured interview to weed out the greedy, the liars, the psychopathic, and the egotists before they get into medical school? But there are elements of those traits in all of us—would there be anyone left? Perhaps we could then use the same process when hiring hospital administrators, whose motives for doing what they do are very obscure to most of us.

Notes

1. Steven Levitt and Stephen Dubner, *Superfreakonomics* (New York: Morrow/HarperCollins, 2009).

2. Christopher Boyce, Gordon Brown, and Simon Moore, "Money and Happiness: Rank of Income, Not Income, Affects Life Satisfaction," *Psychological Science* 21 (2010): 471–75. The finding that money does not buy happiness is hardly new, but the interesting conclusion from this study is that relative wealth may be an important factor in your happiness. Does this have implications for the downfall of communism?

℞ 6

The Elsewhere General Syndrome

Teaching institutionalized arrogance

We were good. We knew we were good. We had to be good, as we were dealing with life-and-death situations daily. But we were no better than we thought we were. I am referring to the team of professionals that I was privileged to be a part of at the University of Western Ontario and University Hospital in London who were doing work in liver transplantation in the 1980s. At one point, we were one of only four programs in the world that had been successful in saving the lives of people dying of liver failure with this dramatic, new, and challenging surgery, and were the only centre in Canada. To further impress the reader, I can relate that among the numerous honours that team received, two of these pioneers, Dr. Stiller and Dr. Wall, have been awarded the Order of Canada for their work in transplantation medicine and organ donation. You might assume that this team was carefully assembled and that the success took years of careful planning by brilliant administrators. If so, you would be wrong.

Like most groundbreaking work in science generally, and in medicine more specifically, this program developed more by happenstance than by careful planning. Some background history is necessary. In discussing institutionalized arrogance, it seems appropriate to do some institutional name-dropping. Dr. Bill Wall, a medical school classmate of mine, was sent by the Department of Surgery to study with world-famous transplant surgeon Sir Roy Calne at Cambridge University in England. At the same time, I arranged to study the medical aspects of liver disease with world-famous hepatologist Gerald Klatskin—one of the few greats of medicine who lived up to his reputation—at Yale University in New Haven, Connecticut. I did not know what Dr. Wall was doing, and he did not know what I was doing. My acceptance at Yale was a fluke of good timing and, strangely enough, I have Richard Nixon to thank for it. In 1974, in one of his many piques of rage at the Eastern Ivy League elite, he impounded the National Institute of Health training grants going to the Ivy League schools. Suddenly, as a foreigner, I had no American competitors for the much-coveted training position. I obtained a Canadian Liver Foundation Fellowship and was accepted for two years of training at Yale. It was no great feat to get that fellowship, either—the Canadian Liver Foundation, with the support of the future British Lord of Crossharbour, Conrad Black, had in its infancy just established a fellowship program to train hepatologists, and I was the first and only applicant that year. They saw this as an opportunity to boast about a Yale-trained Canadian that they had supported. They accepted my application in spite of my rather meagre qualifications.

When Dr. Wall and I arrived back in London in 1977 and became reacquainted, we were also reintroduced to Dr. Calvin Stiller, a man with incredible enthusiasm for transplantation and an equally enormous talent in raising funds, political arm-twisting, and raising media awareness. He almost single-handedly designed, raised funds for, and saw to completion the building of the Multi-Organ Transplant Unit at University Hospital. This was in the face of considerable institutional opposition from various departments within the hospital. There were many who did not share the vision of a benefit to organ transplantation and viewed it as a futile resource-intensive, wasteful endeavour. I initially shared some of those reservations, but by default became the transplant hepatologist, with no training in transplantation or immunology, learning on the job. By the late 1980s, we gladly accepted patients from across the country and from as far away as Australia and Japan and were delighted that the world-famous Toronto Hospital for Sick Children sent us children who needed transplants that were not available there. It is a tribute to the integrity of Dr. Jim Weber of Toronto's Hospital for Sick Children that he sent his small patients to London, recognizing that neither treatment at

Sick Children's nor at the equally famous Toronto General Hospital would save their lives.

Dr. Wall is an unassuming, kind, and considerate surgeon with unequalled precision and judgment in the operating room and on the wards of the hospital, whose brilliant career has been marred only slightly by petty complaints about his impatience with those of lesser surgical talent. We worked hard, earning each other's mutual respect, often in the middle of the night, and often without any precedents, guidelines, or experience to tell us what to do in unique circumstances. We took care to acknowledge the very hard work of a host of highly skilled and dedicated anesthesiologists, intensive care specialists, nurses, social workers, physiotherapists, and dietitians, without whose skills and dedication our work would not have been possible; nevertheless, they were often not given the credit they deserved. Most of those early transplant patients would have died on the operating table were it not for the uncanny, almost instinctive, interventions of anesthesiologist Dr. Judith Kutt, a name few of those early patients will even recall. She did not follow any protocol in this (see Chapter 11). It is somewhat humbling to realize that although there are now six other Canadian liver transplant programs, the one in London is still as good as ever, after my retirement from it.

We failed in some other ways besides not giving enough time in the spotlight to our team members. We joined others in academic medicine in an attitude that was then and still is all too prevalent in all medical teaching centres: an institutionalized attitude that I call the Elsewhere General Syndrome. By this I mean that we and almost everyone around us often came to regard the care that our patients received in other centres as somehow not just different, but inferior to that which we provided. I certainly did my share to transmit this syndrome. None of this was deliberate or mean-spirited, but was an inevitable by-product of the environment we were working in. We had the constant gratitude of patients who were given a second chance after others had given up on them. We had all of the adjectives that are still used by self-promoting businesses everywhere applied to us—groundbreaking, cutting-edge, first, world-class, and of course "centre of excellence." To my knowledge, there has never been a new facility named the "Centre of

Mediocrity," or the "Periphery of Excellence." For simplicity, although not strictly correct, I use the terms "academic centre," "teaching hospital," and "tertiary care centre" interchangeably here.

There is, of course, a grain of truth to the perception of both professionals and the public, both inside and outside academic teaching centres, that the care in teaching hospitals is better than that in what is often referred to derisively as the periphery or "elsewhere general." It is easy to see how this perception is perpetuated. If your gallbladder surgery goes smoothly in a peripheral hospital, you will never be seen by a surgical resident. If, however, your surgery is botched in that peripheral hospital, you will likely be sent to a teaching hospital where the problem will be fixed amid numerous comments by teachers and residents about how incompetent the surgeon out there must have been. If the same procedure is botched in the teaching hospital, there is less likely to be any criticism of the senior surgical professor by the subordinate residents, nurses, or other staff within the teaching centre. It is easy to see why these trainees come to regard "the periphery" as an inferior place to practise.

The elsewhere general syndrome spreads easily and is not confined to medical personnel. This institutional mindset spills over into fundraising efforts and to the general public. Hospital administrators and politicians happily promote the elsewhere general syndrome as well. Every time they open a new "Centre of Excellence" to great media fanfare, they are sending the subtle message that the care provided elsewhere must be somehow less than excellent. At times, the message is far from subtle—the advertisements that waft across the Detroit River for the various health-care facilities in Detroit seem, and probably are, designed to make the nearby Canadians feel that they must cross the river to get good care. In London, which is well known for its biggest industry, health care, local politicians and local media are very reluctant to question the conventional wisdom that London hospitals are better than those in the periphery.

The syndrome is transmitted by word of mouth. No amount of handwashing will interrupt its transmission, and face masks will only distort the message, like a mutation in a virus. Any medical trainee's education is incomplete without being infected. It may start when a neurosurgeon wonders out loud to a junior trainee about why the elsewhere general doctor failed to diagnose the unusual headache as due to a ruptured brain aneurysm, or the hepatologist criticizes the elsewhere general investigations and treatment of the patient with a mysterious or rare cause of cirrhosis that has been misdiagnosed elsewhere. The syndrome will gain virulence throughout the trainee's stay within a teaching hospital, to the point that by the end of the training, she is likely to be convinced that elsewhere general is not a safe or desirable place to practise. The oral transmission of this syndrome, whether via overheard indiscreet elevator conversations or in case presentations at teaching rounds, infects other staff, patients, visitors, and eventually the whole community surrounding an academic teaching hospital. At one point, many years ago, a large banner above the front entrance of University Hospital read, "You are in the right place now," an explicit expression of the elsewhere general syndrome, implying that if you were anywhere else you were in the wrong place. That was removed only at the insistence of Dr. Wall.

The tacit assumption in this elsewhere general syndrome mentality is that those of us in the academic centre know better what is good for the patient than they do out in the periphery or at elsewhere general. Because we may have surgeons who are expert at robotic surgery on beating hearts, we assume that we also have better radiology equipment, better radiologists, and better pathologists, better social workers, better rehabilitation specialists, etc. Those are big assumptions.

There are many unfortunate negative consequences of the elsewhere general syndrome, besides the growth of outsized egos within university teaching hospitals. The first of these has been referred to above—the reluctance of trainees to leave the "centre of excellence" to practise in "the periphery" or at elsewhere general. When I was preparing to retire, I tried hard, to no avail, to get any one of a large number of hospital-based hepatologists to take over my office practice, which had a wide referral base and several thousand patients being seen annually or more frequently. I was even willing to give the practice away to facilitate continuity of care, but no one was interested. Now that I have referred many of those patients to those same individuals at various hospital sites for ongoing care, they are prone to complain that there is no clinic space in the hospital to see them all. At least I can understand that—restrictions of all kinds in the hospital environment were one of the reasons I moved my outpatient practice out of the hospital for the latter part of my career.

The second unfortunate consequence of the elsewhere general syndrome is that, because of the ingrown culture of the academic centres, it is common to assume when a patient arrives that what has been done at elsewhere general is inappropriate, inferior, or incomplete, without considering what could and could not be done there. Although the first priority is to review laboratory, x-ray, and pathology reports from elsewhere general, it is almost automatic to request the biopsies and imaging studies (usually now sent on a CD) at the teaching centre, on the assumption that *our* radiologists, *our* pathologists, and *our* other specialists are likely to provide more useful information. That may or may not be true.

Third, and perhaps worse, is the habit of unnecessarily and automatically repeating all the tests that have already been done, because our protocols, which are assumed to be better than those at elsewhere general, call for that (see Chapter 11). When the process was reversed and it was necessary for me to transfer the care of patients to another tertiary care centre, in Toronto, for example, it was quite annoying to read the reports that came back outlining the plans to repeat every test that had already been done and that had been included with the referral letter. It must be equally upsetting for a referring doctor at elsewhere general to see the same thing happening when the referred patient is first seen at the tertiary care centre.

Fourth, because the syndrome infects the public and patients as well as health-care personnel, it is common for people to drive long distances to the emergency room of tertiary care centres, whether or not they need tertiary care, without giving their local physician or emergency room a chance to treat their perceived emergency. The elsewhere general discussions on the wards of tertiary care centres undoubtedly contribute to this inappropriate use of resources.

Fifth, in an academic teaching centre far removed from family and a family doctor, severely ill patients with no hope of survival often have endless tests and treatments that amount to nothing more than straightening the deck chairs on a sinking ship, all because the prevalent endemic elsewhere general syndrome convinces everyone to never question that we can do what others cannot. Because of its teaching role and a multiplicity of specialists, a patient in a tertiary care centre is likely to get more fragmented care, without anyone looking at the big picture. Multiple specialists deal with small aspects of the patient's overall care, while no one assumes the traditional role of the family doctor to direct overall care. The case of a friend's mother illustrates this process well. At ninety-six and demented, she was admitted to a tertiary care centre with sudden deterioration. Her daughter, who had no medical training, diagnosed the terminal stroke, while the expert medical team suggested that her deterioration was due to a urinary tract infection. They nevertheless subjected her to two computed tomography scans of her head and only her daughter's intervention spared her the pain of having a lumbar puncture to exclude meningitis a few days before she died.

Finally, the elsewhere general syndrome makes physicians in "the periphery" reluctant to provide even routine care to patients who have had advanced treatments at a teaching centre lest the specialists criticize that care. It is true that one needs to be cautious about drug interactions when prescribing medication for transplant patients who are taking drugs to prevent organ rejection. But it is not true that the transplant nephrologist or hepatologist should be responsible for treating the arthritis, the ingrown toenails, or the hair loss of the patient simply because he has done a great job of replacing a failed organ. I always found it frustrating to have to advise patients about aspects of their care that I knew nothing about, simply because both they and their primary care provider regarded their health after transplant as so precarious that only a transplant physician could do anything for them.

Academic centres thrive on this culture of institutionalized arrogance. However, many academic centre staff are academic staff because of their research and teaching skills, not for their skills or interest in caring for real people. To many faculty in university teaching centres, the few months each year spent "on service," i.e., caring for patients, is viewed as an inconvenient price they have to pay to maintain their academic rank; they would much rather be treating experimental rats. Writing research grant proposals, classroom teaching, and administrative duties all compete with caring for the patients in a teaching hospital. The faculty member's interest and dedication to the patient whom they see once or twice is certainly different than that of the family doctor of that patient in a distant city or town.

The consequences of the elsewhere general syndrome are not confined to a waste of resources and fragmentation of care and misperceptions; they can be downright dangerous. To illustrate this, a recent case study will suffice. A patient whose ultrasound at elsewhere general was reported to show a large liver tumour had his liver reassessed with magnetic resonance imaging at a tertiary care centre. When that was reported to show no tumour, he was told he had no tumour, without further consideration about who was right and who was wrong. If he in fact does have a tumour, the tertiary care centre has done him a gross disservice. If or when he comes back to the teaching centre with malignancy that has spread to other organs, there will likely be a different team of specialists that are "on service" who will be hesitant to criticize the initial clinical team or the radiologists who concluded that he had no tumour. They are, after all, part of the teaching faculty.

There is no easy cure for the elsewhere general syndrome. In many ways, it becomes a matter of better communication and understanding of what other centres are capable of doing. In some cases, small changes would reap enormous benefits. A courtesy phone call to the appropriate referring physician after the operation unfortunately is a rarity today. The electronic patient record, for example, has not yet lived up to its potential for various reasons. Health records departments of at least some teaching hospitals do not record the name and fax number of the referring physician in their electronic record database if that physician is outside of their usual geographic area, making it very difficult to keep track of who the home community primary caregiver is. When I send a patient to one of my colleagues in the teaching hospital, I usually get a good detailed consultation note back, but it is seldom copied to the family doctor who sent the patient to me. Many times, if it is a resident dictating the note, she may not realize that I am not the family doctor, and in a busy schedule, taking the time to find out who is the primary caregiver is perceived to be more trouble than it is worth—how could the family doctor be of help in caring for such a complex problem?

The health records department in some teaching hospitals will also not incorporate notes from outside physicians as a part of the electronic record. Concerns of hospital lawyers and property law were the excuses given when I inquired about why my office notes could be kept in the hospital record as a paper document but not as part of the electronic record. I have difficulty understanding what is different about the legal aspects of information on paper as compared to the same information in an electronic format. This policy does not help the resident who can access the electronic record but not the paper record when my patient shows up in the emergency room at three a.m. It is also peculiar that I can review the electronic record of a referred patient in my office only if she has been seen at one of a few local hospitals that are on the same computer system, and then only by paying a monthly fee to the hospital for the access.

Knowing what is done well and where it is done is also a part of the solution. Knowing who is responsible for what part of a patient's overall care is also very necessary, but is seldom spelled out when a patient is discharged from a tertiary care centre. Within insulated ivory tower tertiary care centres, there is a need to educate everyone about the bigger world of medicine, where most of the care of their patients will take place. A compulsory rotation of trainees to several of the referral centres to educate them in the outside world of medicine would be of enormous benefit both to them and to their hosts there.

I have been privileged to work both within an academic teaching centre for many years and then partially in "the periphery" for the last fifteen years of my career, although I was never affiliated with a non-teaching hospital. The latter experience in "the periphery" made me acutely aware of the negative effects of the elsewhere general syndrome. As I prepared to close my practice in preparation for retirement, I was pleasantly surprised to find that many of the patients who had been coming to me for years, often from far away, drawn in part by my previous academic reputation, had completely competent physicians closer to home to care for their complex liver problems. Many patients were reluctant to give up the connection to me, because of the perception that, as I had been associated with a tertiary care centre, the care here had to be better than what they could get close to home. I hope I did not contribute much to that perception, but I am not sure. I did keep the Yale certificate of training on my wall, but not where most patients could see it.

If we are willing to step outside our ivory tower, we will find that the care at non-academic centres is not necessarily inferior, and may be more efficient than that at teaching hospitals, although it is undoubtedly very different. When a relative of mine needed some minor surgery for hammertoes, we could not find an orthopedic surgeon anywhere in London who would do it. We travelled eighty kilometres to elsewhere general to have it done, and it was done very well. It seems no one is training the next generation of orthopedic surgeons to do this menial but very important work at the centre of excellence. That surgeon should be allowed to advertise that he does that surgery, and does it very well, and should be involved in the training of future orthopedic surgeons. He is undoubtedly one of many specialists in the periphery who could and would willingly provide valuable training not available in our teaching hospitals.

Some degree of realistic self-promotion on the part of individuals, programs, and institutions may after all be very necessary to make this complex system of health care function smoothly. We need, however, to avoid the smug and ego-boosting "centre of excellence" jargon. The professionals working in those Centres of Excellence should not, with that designation, be insulated from criticism of the care they provide; nor does that designation give them a licence to propagate the Elsewhere General Syndrome. It is unbecoming to apply superlatives to yourself or your institution; if others apply them, they may really mean something.

7

Social Distance

The famous, the infamous, and the doctor

It seems obvious that Michael Jackson did not get the best medical care that his money could buy but he was not the only rich and famous individual who has received very poor medical care. In the Kennedy White House, the president's personal physician was responsible for prescribing and scouring D.C. pharmacies for ever-increasing amounts of the president's favorite uppers—amphetamines. These are the same stimulants that powered much of the countercultural revolution in the later 1960s and became one of the targets of a later administration's war on drugs. They are still extensively abused. It is clear that JFK was not following his doctor's orders, but that his doctor was following JFK's orders. The same reversal of traditional roles was probably true in the events leading up to Michael Jackson's tragic demise and that of Howard Hughes.

Why do rich and famous individuals frequently receive inferior medical advice and care, when they can afford the best? The answer, at least in part, relates to a sociological phenomenon encompassed in the term "social distance."[1] Social distance is measured on a horizontal axis as distinct from socio-economic status, which is usually conceptualized as a vertical continuum directly related to income. In contrast, social distance is only indirectly related to income, and has more to do with differences in beliefs, values, religion, race, and lifestyle. *Normative* social distance refers to the distinctions we all make, based on what we consider typical or usual "norms," between "us" and "them." *Affective* social distance measures the amount of affection, empathy, or sympathy individuals or groups develop for individuals or groups that are different from them. This construct was originally used by sociologists to measure how well we relate to and tolerate individuals who are very different from us, whether by gender, skin colour, economic status, sexual orientation, or religious or ethnic background. There is extensive literature on social distance as it relates to racial integration, housing, school segregation, and the flight of whites to the suburbs of major U.S. cities in the 1960s. There is little literature about it as it relates to medical care.

The rich and famous are not alone in frequently receiving inferior medical care. At the other end of the socio-economic spectrum, the poor and destitute are also less likely than the middle classes to receive optimal care. This undoubtedly relates to the social distance between them and their physicians. Some studies show that physicians spend less time with those of a lower socio-economic status.[2] Women with coronary artery disease are likely to have interventional surgery recommended to them at a later stage of the disease than men, with resultant poorer outcomes.[3] The disparities are not explained by any differences in the ability to pay for the care. Although such studies are often cited as evidence of a gender or racial bias on the part of the physicians, it would be more appropriate to consider them in the context of the broader dimension of social distance between the patient and physician. Social distance factors may also have been involved in the slow initial response of the medical establishment to the AIDS epidemic. Early cases were almost all homosexual men with multiple partners, a group at a considerable social distance from most physicians and researchers.

Whenever someone visits a physician, there is a complex social interaction as well as a medical one. Social distance affects that interaction as does "asymmetry of power," another concept that refers to an imbalance of power in an interaction, whether medical or social. Unlike normative social distance between two individuals, which changes very little under different circumstances, asymmetry of power varies with the circumstances of the encounter. To illustrate: Under usual circumstances, physicians are in an asymmetric power position when interacting with nurses, as they give nurses orders. However, if those orders include an inappropriate request—such as to check a patient's vital signs hourly all night—a senior nurse can readily assume a subtle, relative position of power and have the junior resident called hourly all night with trivial reports that could well wait until daylight. Anyone who has ever taken calls in a hospital has experienced some such reversal of the usual power asymmetry.

Much has also been written about the potential for sexual exploitation or abuse of patients by their physicians because of the power asymmetry in the examining room, and the real need to examine real bodies that is an integral part of the physician–patient encounter. The regulatory authorities have established guidelines to avoid "crossing boundaries" and interacting with patients in a non-professional manner. Some of these seem designed, under the guise of professionalism, to maintain the paternalism and the asymmetry of power that is an integral part of any medical encounter. However, nothing can get a doctor in trouble with the College of Physicians and Surgeons faster than using the temporary asymmetric position of power to inappropriately examine a private part of a patient. At times, fear of such complaints leads to inferior care. In my practice, when women of a different ethnic background visited me and I was uncertain what they expected during the physical examination, I often erred on the side of caution, possibly at times missing some important abnormality that should have been noted and treated. Their care was perhaps compromised because of this.

In any health-care encounters, the combination of asymmetry of power factors and social distance factors has consequences for both individuals that varies in different circumstances. A military surgeon may not care whether the patient is one of ours or one of theirs; his job is to patch up the wounds and get the soldier out of the hospital. The social distance and asymmetry of power is much more important if an obstetrician working in the same war zone is trying to provide advice about good antenatal nutrition and encourage breast-feeding. When the patient is a convict serving time in a federal prison, the social distance and power asymmetry is at one extreme. The patient is socially distant from the doctor and deprived of almost any power. He is likely to have not only an abbreviated encounter but also very little input into the decisions made about his care. The other extreme is reached when the patient has, or is perceived to have, all the power and again may be socially distant from the doctor, but in the opposite direction. When Michael J. Fox was visited by the neurosurgeon, in his Boston hotel room, the night before his stereotactic brain surgery for his presumed Parkinson's disease, it is clear that Fox was the major decision-maker as to what should be done. Few neurosurgeons do house calls to hotel rooms—unless the patient is rich and famous and calling the shots.

When the power distribution is equal and the social distance between the doctor and the patient is short, the latter is likely to get the best care. To make this as equal as possible, it is necessary for both parties in a medical encounter to recognize the possible consequences of the asymmetry of power and social distances. It may be very easy to dismiss the request of the ex-convict for treatment of his hepatitis C because the physician cannot relate to the patient's past experiences, values, and beliefs in the same way as he can to the same request of a school principal—there is a greater affective social distance between the physician and the ex-convict than between him and the school principal. It is no accident that the first celebrated heart transplant patient was a dentist, a health-care professional at a short social distance from the then relatively obscure cardiovascular surgeon Dr. Christiaan Barnard.

On one end of the social distance scale, it may be very difficult for a physician to be objective and to resist an inappropriate request for unnecessary treatment if the patient is socially powerful, famous, or rich. I wish Steve Jobs well with his liver transplant for an unusual pancreatic cancer that had spread to his liver, a borderline indication for liver transplantation that would not be recommended in many transplant centres. However, I do not envy those caring for him who must have had to deal with enormous pressure in making an objective decision about what was best for him. Or did they make the decision at all?

I have been largely spared any undue pressures in caring for the rich or famous although I would certainly be considered socially distant from them. I am sure some of my patients were rich and famous, but I was usually too naïve to recognize them as such. I did spend a short time working as a locum in a Middle East emirate, but only toward the end of my stay recognized the code on the corner of the charts designating the patient as a member of the royal family. I undoubtedly treated several members of the royal family there without even acknowledging their royal status.

The case of Dr. Michael DeBakey and his aortic aneurysm is interesting to analyze from the social distance perspective. This renowned cardiac surgeon, aged ninety-seven and still working, although not performing surgery, developed a dissection of the aorta, which he diagnosed himself. The surgery for this had been developed and perfected years before by him, and he had taught the very renowned cardiac surgeons who performed the operation on him when he was desperately ill in coma. As well as being his former pupils, they were also personal friends with their famous patient. The social distance between them, apart from age, was probably shorter than that between most pairs of identical twins. They also, however, at the insistence of his much younger wife, disregarded his explicit advance directive (see Chapter 9) in proceeding with the surgery, which was a technical success and kept him alive for almost two years. It is little wonder that their press releases emphasized the irrelevance of age in the decision to perform the operation—that was the only social distance factor that made them at all different from him. It is also true that no other ninety-seven-year-old who developed this condition has ever been operated on for it. Was the social distance between the patient and the caregivers so short that, in this situation, the latter could not bring themselves to honour his wishes with respect to resuscitation, endowing the patient with the change of directive that any of them thought they would make in his situation?

I was more concerned, during my thirty-three years in practice, with the social distance between myself and many addicts, mentally ill, or homeless patients. When a new patient was jokingly referred to as NOSP by the clinic staff, I immediately knew that I would have a struggle to find any empathy or commonality with that patient. "NOSP" is a colloquialism standing for "Not Our Sort of Person," or "Not Our Sort of People," and is a nearly perfect description of someone at a great normative social distance from the speaker. It conveys a tremendous amount of information in one non-word about both the subject and the speaker. It was often necessary to discuss the problems of NOSPs in blunt street language that would be considered non-professional by the

College, and to discuss things completely unrelated to medicine in a search for any element of common ground to relate to them at all. A surprising number of my alcoholic and drug-addicted patients decided I was a real human being they could relate to, and accept some advice from, only when we swapped stories about fly fishing or some other activity unrelated to medicine.

When one considers the concepts of power asymmetry and social distances, as they relate to medical care, other common terms used in this context become problematic as well. "Doctors' orders" is one such term. Richard Nixon was allowed to stay in California and recuperate "on doctors' orders" in November 1974, when ordered by a judge to appear in court in Washington D.C. Although the obliging doctors were ordered by the court to examine the ex-president, they concluded that he was unfit to travel or even to give a deposition from his home in San Clemente. Such doctors' orders do not come in a neutral vacuum with no consideration of the context from individuals unaware of the consequences of their decisions. One would like to think the doctors were being objective in ordering him to stay in bed in California, but it is difficult to see how his phlebitis and pulmonary embolism would prevent him from providing a deposition, or would be worsened by lying on a bed in an airplane for a few hours rather than where he no doubt preferred to be–lying in bed at home.

When the patient is in a more powerful social position than the doctor, the doctor's orders tend to become the patient's orders. There is no doubt that John F. Kennedy was ordering his doctor to get him his amphetamines rather than the doctor ordering them for him because of medical indications. Except for in-hospital settings where doctor's orders are carried out by a third party, such as a nurse, doctor's orders should usually be more properly called doctor's suggestions or doctor's recommendations. This at least makes the patient a participant in the decision-making process, although giving the patient too much decision-making choice can increase the anxiety level inherent in any medical decision-making, as shown by Barry Schwartz.[4]

Another prevalent term in medical parlance is "compliance," i.e., the adherence to a regimen of care, whether taking of medications as prescribed, sticking to a prescribed diet, adhering to a physiotherapy routine, or complying with a recommendation to stop drinking. This too is intimately connected to the social distance between the patient and the physician. If the patient is on a social par with the doctor (a short social distance away), there is likely to be some detailed discussion of the rationale for the regimen advised by the doctor; an explanation of the importance of compliance has been demonstrated to increase adherence in a variety of settings. Physicians often request office visits and do blood tests to measure drug levels, including alcohol, just to determine whether or not the patient is taking medication as ordered, or at least following the recommended routine. I suspect that physicians are more likely to question and test the compliance of individuals who are socially distant from themselves.

It is easy to assume that the patient who is a prostitute, and therefore socially distant from the doctor, is not going to be compliant. This then becomes a self-fulfilling prophecy, as there is likely to be less explanation given to her about the importance of taking all of the prescribed antibiotic doses. Because physicians spend less time examining and talking to patients who are socially distant from themselves, non-compliance inevitably increases. In the extreme situation of inmates in prison and in certain mental institutions, attempts by discussion to increase compliance with taking medication are simply abandoned by the expeditious use of nurses who are ordered to watch the patient swallow every dose of every prescribed medication. This can be effective but does nothing to ensure compliance once the patient is out of the corrections facility or the mental institution. Rather than spending less time discussing the importance of adherence or compliance with those who are socially distant from themselves, physicians should ideally recognize the social distance barriers to compliance and spend more time with those who are more likely, because of social circumstances, to be non-compliant.

Being labelled as non-compliant by a health-care worker can have a very negative impact on one's future care. In the extreme cases with which I worked, non-compliance was one of the frequent major reasons for denying very sick liver patients an opportunity to have a life-saving liver transplant. Non-compliance is not, however, an all-or-nothing phenomenon, and at times can be quite healthy. If a knowledgeable and reasonable patient refuses to undergo a procedure recommended by a physician who may have monetary motives for the recommendation (see Chapter 5), that patient may incorrectly be labelled as non-compliant, and that label is likely to adversely affect her subsequent care. The label should be applied only to those who are persistently non-compliant after detailed and repeated explanations of the reasons for the recommendations. Unfortunately, such individuals are numerous and tragic and usually at such a great social distance from anyone in the health-care field that no amount of talking will alter their self-destructive non-compliance.

Two other phenomena come into play when there is a considerable social distance between the physician and the patient. These are what Malcolm Gladwell[5] refers to as choking and panicking. Although sometimes resulting in the same poor outcome, they are really opposite psychological phenomena, both resulting from stress. Choking is a loss of instinctive behaviour under stress; panicking is reversion to *only* instinctive behaviour when stressed. There can be little doubt that caring for a rich and famous patient is a stressful situation for a physician, and both phenomena may come into play.

According to his autobiography,[6] Michael J. Fox, at age twenty-nine, was told on the first day he consulted an esteemed neurologist that he had Parkinson's disease. Did that neurologist get it right or did he choke or panic because he was seeing a rich and famous Hollywood star? The instinctive response for a relaxed and competent neurologist seeing a less famous patient with apparent Parkinson's disease starting at age twenty-nine would have been to consider other possibilities, including Wilson disease. However, if that neurologist choked or panicked, the result might be the same, as panicking is associated with a narrowing of perceptions, which in this situation might lead to a failure to consider other possible diagnoses. I have often wondered if anyone along the way has considered the old medical adage that anyone under age forty with Parkinson's disease has Wilson disease until proven otherwise. Wilson disease is a rare genetic disorder of copper metabolism, diagnosed with a careful eye examination and tests of urine and blood that could not be done on a single day. It seems very unlikely almost twenty years later that Michael J. Fox has been misdiagnosed, with multiple neurologists and a neurosurgeon all involved in his care. But if the elsewhere general syndrome (see Chapter 6) was in effect at that initial brief encounter, no one may have ever thought to question the diagnosis. The tremors and rigidity of a Hollywood star are none of my business, but for the sake of Michael J. Fox and the Michael J. Fox Foundation for Parkinson's Research, I hope he is not raising money for research to cure a disease that he does not have, or is missing being appropriately medicated for a treatable disease he does have.

Perhaps one of the biggest problems facing the rich and famous, besides the loss of any privacy and anonymity, is accessing good medical care. In this they have something in common with social outcasts, criminals, the destitute, and the homeless. As I review the problem of social distance as it relates to medical care, it makes me grateful to realize that I will never be rich or famous and hopefully will never be destitute or homeless.

Notes

1. The original social distance scale was described by Emory S. Bogardus in 1925. There have been numerous adaptations used in social science studies since that time.
2. S. Willems, S. De Maesschalck, M. Deveugele, et al., "Socio-economic Status of the Patient and Doctor-Patient Communication: Does It Make a Difference?" *The American Journal of Medicine* 56 (2005): 139–46.
3. S.S. Khan, S. Nessim, R. Gray, et al., "Increased Mortality of Women in Coronary Artery Bypass Surgery: Evidence for Referral Bias," *Annals of Internal Medicine,* vol. 112, no. 8 (1990): 561–67.
4. B. Schwartz, *The Paradox of Choice* (New York: Harper Perennial, 2004).
5. M. Gladwell, *What the Dog Saw* (New York: Little, Brown and Company, 2009).
6. M.J. Fox, *Lucky Man* (New York: Hyperion, 2002).

Rx 8

Medical Lingo

Dangerous doctor-speak

The resident who came to my office recently was reviewing the progress of several patients I was following with her in the hospital. "Mrs. Brown went into honk yesterday," she announced with considerable concern. I scratched my bald head and tried to jolt my memory centre to recall anything about honk, although I was pretty sure it should be spelled with capitals—"HONK." That process failed, and I stalled for time, trying to get some clues about HONK, not yet ready to admit that I did not know what it stood for. "Did you get her out of it successfully?" I asked. She confirmed that the endocrinology service had dealt with it and that the patient had indeed gotten out of HONK. I knew Mrs. Brown was diabetic and with that clue about endocrinology, guessed that HONK had to be related to her diabetes. As I put the letters together I realized that it must have something to do with a high blood sugar, and finally guessed that HONK had to be **h**yperosmolar **n**on-**k**etotic something or other—likely diabetic coma. But why was it not HONKC if that was what the acronym stood for? Or HYPNOKCO?

This is just one example of medical lingo that has proliferated to the point that even the most up-to-date and knowledgeable physicians are often unfamiliar with the terms their colleagues use every day. People no longer have heart attacks or coronary occlusions—they have STEMIs or non-STEMIs, depending on whether or not the ST segment of the standard electrocardiogram (ECG) is elevated at the time of the coronary event. STEMI is an acronym for **ST** segment **e**levation **m**yocardial **i**nfarction. Depending on the circumstances of your heart attack, it may be treated by PCA (percutaneous coronary angioplasty), or perhaps by having a CABAG. This is pronounced *cabbage,* but is a bit more complicated than eating some vegetables—although if you eat your vegetables, it might prevent or delay the need for a CABAG, which stands for *coronary artery bypass graft*. Although the name has changed, the condition has not, and the lingo is unlikely to lead to any confusion in this example

ARDS is a more problematic acronym, as it may be variously used to mean *acute respiratory distress syndrome*, or *adult respiratory distress syndrome*. This term does not indicate anything about the cause of the respiratory failure, which for either type of ARDS could be a wide variety of diseases ranging from liver failure to severe infections to trauma. Designating someone as having ARDS without clarifying the meaning often diverts the attention of treating specialists away from the underlying cause to treating the symptom.

Many medical acronyms are well established and universally understood, with a long history and a solid basis for their use. Among the best of these are the officially recognized eponyms and acronyms that facilitate communication and shorten the length of letters and notes in health records. There are literally hundreds of these, from those honouring the discoverer of a disease or of a physical sign such as a Trendelenburg gait, to those that simply describe features of an illness that usually show up together. Some, such as trisomy 21, also known as "Down's syndrome" after the physician who provided the most detailed early description of the features of this genetic disorder, have a solid scientific basis. Sadly, political correctness has now overruled the designation of this as belonging to Down as the first describer, and it is now officially called *Down syndrome*. The same process has led to Wilson disease instead of Wilson's disease for the disorder of copper metabolism described by Kinnear Wilson in 1912, and to Cushing syndrome rather than Cushing's syndrome for the disorder of cortisol metabolism described by Harvey Cushing in the same year. Dropping the possessives seems not only to entail some loss of esteem for the keen observers who first described them, but also to be applied in a haphazard way. It is not clear to me why the nomenclature gurus decided, for example, that the virus causing mononucleosis syndrome would be called Epstein-Barr virus, but the cardiac malformation described by Ebstein would be called

Ebstein's anomaly. And the downloadable Eponyms package that I use contains over 1,300 entries, with an almost equal number listed with possessives and non-possessives.

Much of the jargon in medical records and discussion are of little significance as long as it does not create confusion that could harm the patient. A doctor who is confused about the terms being applied to your condition could become very dangerous to your health, unless she takes the time to clarify what the terms mean. Describing the patient who went into HONK is probably not in this category. Although terms such as HONK are likely to confuse the layperson and non-specialist alike, they are unlikely to do the patient any harm, even if the treating physician is not familiar with the latest faddish name for what he is treating.

In another recent case, an intensive care chart entry by a neurologist at the hospital where I was working concluded that the patient did not yet fulfill criteria for PRESS. At least he did not say the patient *went into* PRESS. Not having any clue as to what PRESS stood for, I had no idea what to do about the possibility that the patient might have it. I was certainly familiar with the possibility that the drugs I was giving the patient could produce some brain dysfunction, and was concerned that the confusion and tremors she had were due to what I knew as CPM. As I investigated, it became clear that both I and the neurologist were concerned about the same thing—we just knew it by different names. PRESS stands for posterior reversible encephalopathy syndrome (why the second "s"?), also known by the even more confusing RPLS (reversible posterior leukoencephalopathy syndrome), and is usually detected with magnetic resonance imaging (MRI). CPM stands for central pontine myelinolysis and is usually diagnosed by computed tomography scanning (CT). As the diagnostic technology used in brain imaging changed, so did the name of the findings. Those who are more attuned to etiology than to imaging may call the same spectrum of clinical findings I refer to as CPM, and the neurologist referred to as PRESS by even other names such as ODM (osmotic demyelination syndrome) or, in the right setting, CNI-induced neurotoxicity, CNI standing for calcineurin-inhibitor, a class of drugs used to prevent organ rejection. With all these names, is it any wonder that it is often not just the patient who gets confused?

The rationale behind other shortcuts and abbreviations do not need to be fully understood to be appreciated and acted upon appropriately. Even an orthopedic surgeon can understand that a report of a "wandering P wave" on an ECG signifies some significant heart rhythm disturbance and not some confused patient with a urinary tract problem. He does not need to appreciate that the reason for the P-Q-R-S-T-U designation of the waveform components of the ECG dates back to Descartes' use in the 1600s of zero as the origin point of his Cartesian coordinates, and the letters of the first half of the alphabet for various mathematical functions, leaving only those of the second half of the alphabet to describe the features of the new-fangled electrocardiogram (x, y, and z were already taken to describe the three dimensions on a graph).

Likewise, one does not need to know what the peculiar and largely arbitrary acronyms used by drug companies for the studies they sponsor even stand for—the meat is in the final reports. However, some of these contrived and often inane acronyms are really quite amusing, and some are potentially problematic, not because they are confusing, but because of their implied messages. The HALT–C Trial, which was designed to determine whether or not long-term antiviral treatment would prevent the progression of hepatitis C stood for hepatitis C antiviral long-term treatment against cirrhosis. Another study, called the CURE study, CURE standing for clopidogrel in unstable angina to prevent recurrent events, has been criticized because of the subtle coercive implication that the sponsor's drug provides a cure for the problem of unstable angina. How many of the more than 12,000 trial subjects agreed to enter the study because the name implied that they might be cured? The people in sponsoring pharmaceutical companies who come up with these acronyms for studies do so with some consideration of the appeal to the potential subjects. HALT–C has similar subliminal appeal built into the name, although in this case the final conclusion was that the treatment failed to halt the progression of hepatitis C.

While some medical lingo is quite helpful and other terms are quite innocuous, some can be at least annoying and confusing, if not downright dangerous. The psychiatrist who refers to the patient's SAD may be discussing a seasonal affective disorder, or a more serious schizoaffective disorder. This is not likely to be a problem if he is the only one who refers to the note later, although all physicians have had the experience of looking at their own notes later and wondering what they were saying. The gastroenterologist who discusses the possibility of CD in notes may be referring to either Crohn's disease or celiac disease. The term IBD (inflammatory bowel disease) is often used to avoid the need to carefully assess which of two common inflammatory bowel diseases the patient has and can easily be confused with the equally vague IBS, which refers to irritable bowel syndrome. Use of the latter term also avoids the need to be specific about symptoms, as IBS conveniently is used to refer to a host of gastrointestinal symptoms including excessive flatulence, bloating, abdominal pain, nausea, and diarrhea or constipation or both. It is little wonder that patients with this disease are among the least satisfied with the care they get once they are labelled with IBS; most physicians stop dealing with the symptoms, regarding this as not a real anatomical disease that requires real treatment.

It is when the use of shortcuts becomes second nature to physicians that the real dangers arise. The health records of inpatients are replete with detailed, legible, and grammatically correct handwritten notes by nurses, physiotherapists, dietitians, and social workers, often even using complete sentences. In contrast, medical staff notes, apart from being notoriously illegible, are so riddled with incomplete words, abbreviations, and nonexistent words as to become almost useless to anyone else involved in treating or caring for the patient. At times, one gets the distinct impression that jargon is used to deliberately obfuscate. The use of complete sentences is rare and numbers are scribbled on an irregular line diagram to designate, for example, blood counts, electrolyte values, blood gases, or settings on the ventilator. The absence of many things, symptoms, signs, imaging studies, or other investigations is usually designated by a 0 and anything that is considered normal is designated with an N. These are handy, appropriate, and universally understood shortcuts, but by abandoning proper sentences and grammar, they also encourage the use of other abbreviations that can lead to confusion.

Lest the reader think that I am exaggerating about the extent of this problem, I have copied here an actual consultation note that a resident I was working with recently handed me after completing the request for consultation. This was not an incompetent resident with a poor grasp of English, but a highly competent senior resident who was about to complete his training. The record has no need to be altered for confidentiality—it is impossible to identify the patient's name at the top, and equally impossible to identify the resident from the illegible signature of the resident at the bottom.

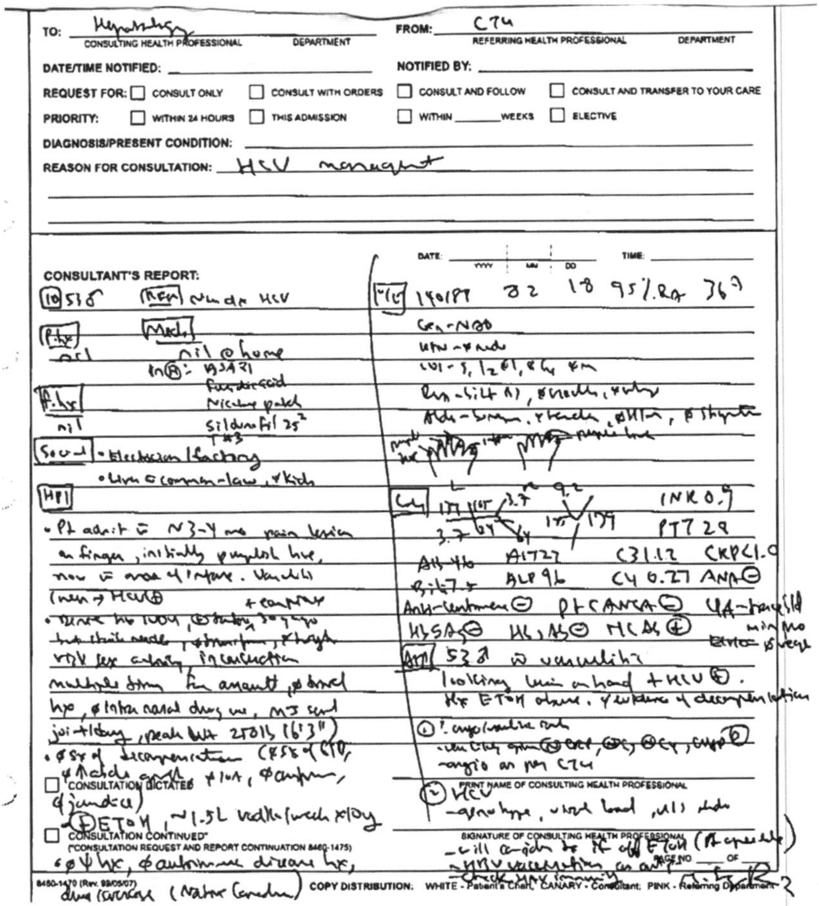
TO: CONSULTING HEALTH PROFESSIONAL DEPARTMENT
FROM: REFERRING HEALTH PROFESSIONAL DEPARTMENT
DATE/TIME NOTIFIED:
NOTIFIED BY:
REQUEST FOR: ☐ CONSULT ONLY ☐ CONSULT WITH ORDERS ☐ CONSULT AND FOLLOW ☐ CONSULT AND TRANSFER TO YOUR CARE
PRIORITY: ☐ WITHIN 24 HOURS ☐ THIS ADMISSION ☐ WITHIN ____ WEEKS ☐ ELECTIVE
DIAGNOSIS/PRESENT CONDITION:
REASON FOR CONSULTATION:
DATE: YYYY MM DD TIME:
CONSULTANT'S REPORT:
☐ CONSULTATION DICTATED
☐ CONSULTATION CONTINUED* (*CONSULTATION REQUEST AND REPORT CONTINUATION 8460-1475)
PRINT NAME OF CONSULTING HEALTH PROFESSIONAL
SIGNATURE OF CONSULTING HEALTH PROFESSIONAL
PAGE NO ___ OF ___
8460-1470 (Rev. 99/05/07)
COPY DISTRIBUTION: WHITE - Patient's Chart, CANARY - Consultant, PINK - Referring Department

It is seldom that I ever express any empathy or sympathy for lawyers, but if or when one requests the complete health record of a patient to prepare litigation or an application to appeal a denied disability claim, and gets something like the above, she would have my sympathy. Try explaining what this says to a judge. More to the point, what information does this kind of writing convey to the physician who requested the specialist's opinion? He may be able, with some squinting and guessing, to conclude that the patient drinks too much alcohol, and does not have evidence of hepatitis B, and may have several purple toes, but what else?

A comparison of the approach to writing of physicians and nurses may be instructive. When I first met my future wife, she was in the process of completing her thesis for a master's degree in nursing. We spent endless not very romantic hours revising, editing, correcting syntax, and formatting her dissertation, at the insistence of the nursing faculty, which at times seemed more concerned with the style than the content. This insistence on proper grammar generally seems to be reflected in nurses' notes in patients' charts. While they may frequently use abbreviations and shortcuts, they are usually confined to well-accepted and readily understood terms—and are even likely to be legible. When a nursing note indicates that the patient *c/o SOB*, it is easy to conclude that she means that the patient *complains of shortness of breath*, and the context will tell the reader that she was not commenting about his personality. In contrast, the physician who enters a note about the SOB, is likely to write that the *JVP= 2 cm*, and that S1, S2 = N, 0 m. Perhaps some nursing faculty should be recruited to teach medical trainees a course on intelligible communication.

There is no easy solution to the problem of unintelligible medical lingo. The face sheet of the discharge form at University Hospital has a bold instruction at the top, warning: "**No Abbreviations Allowed**" but the policy is not enforced. There is a move in the pharmacy world to eliminate handwritten prescriptions altogether and to require that all drug order entries be done electronically. This would reduce the number of medication errors, and should be encouraged. However, these moves do not go far in enhancing communication and understanding between medical practitioners. Several changes in routine practice could provide at least a partial solution.

First, there needs to be a systematic peer audit within teaching hospitals, perhaps of randomly chosen notes, to critique what is being written. This was a common practice twenty years ago, but has largely been abandoned, perhaps because the faculty who now do much of the supervising of trainees hated it so much when they were trainees. It is a common trait of old luddites like the writer to hark back to the good old days when everything was done better, but I cannot understand why this practice was abandoned. After I announced my retirement from the hospital, I offered to develop criteria and do random reviews of discharge summaries and notes with trainees as a teaching exercise, free of charge, but there was no interest in this from the teaching staff.

Second, there should be more use made of typed notes and reports. In the era of electronic records, there is little excuse for any record like the one above to ever appear in a health record. It is highly appropriate to use such note-taking at the bedside to record the data and to organize one's thoughts and to then use that record to enter a rational and concise dictated note for the permanent record, discarding the scribbles. A typed report might even include some proper sentences. The electronic patient record should be able to accommodate this readily. There might even be cost savings and a reduction in paper waste if all progress notes, summary notes, consultation notes, discharge summaries, etc., were typed. One danger, however, does not disappear with dictated notes just because they are legible. If they are not properly reviewed and revised, they can be completely misleading and detrimental to the patient's future care. A critically missed *not* can leave the record with erroneous information that will label the patient as having something she does not, as in, "The patient does admit to intravenous drug use," rather than, "The patient does *not* admit to intravenous drug use." Careful review by the person doing the dictation is necessary even with legible typed reports, and maybe even more so than with illegible scribbles. This should be greatly facilitated with steadily improving voice-recognition technology that allows continuous review by the dictator as he dictates the note.

Third, doctors need to be cautious about using terms that are not a part of standard accepted and widely understood nomenclature, or at least to spell out what their shortened words or acronyms mean the first time they are used. With IT (information technology) advances, it should be possible to "program" a transcriptionist, whether human or electronic, to refuse to type an incomplete word or acronym that does not appear in a standard set of approved terms, unless it was spelled out the first time it was used. If a physician, in training or on staff, got a phone call or e-mail from the transcription services every time they dictated some meaningless string of capital letters that was not in the approved lexicon, it would not only improve the notes and letters, it would also provide valuable teaching feedback. Physicians could certainly learn by paying more attention to the notes written or dictated by other professionals, whether they are the typed notes of their teachers or the legible handwritten notes of nurses.

While the mastery of words used by lawyers, often to obfuscate issues, is not necessary in health records, even physicians could learn something from the precision and care that lawyers use in preparing their briefs. Perhaps if some of the above suggestions were implemented in whole or in part for health records, it would make the job of a litigation lawyer easier as he reviews a medical file. That seems a small price to pay for better communication between physicians.

℞ 9

Exits

Opening the escape hatch debate

Few expressions of medical lingo are as readily recognized by the general public as DNR (do not resuscitate) and its antithesis, CPR (cardiopulmonary resuscitation). These terms, however, are opposite poles of a wide spectrum of possibilities that often create dilemmas in dealing with severely ill patients. Debates focus on the futility of aggressive or high-tech supportive care, quality of life issues, assisted suicide, and who should make the decisions. Health-care workers, families, societies, and even politicians often stake out ideological and inflexible positions. At times, such disputes take on what would be almost comic dimensions if the subject were not so serious. The truth is often buried in rhetoric, as illustrated in the case of Terri Schiavo, whose death in 2005 after seven years of legal wrangling about removal of her feeding tube touched off a national debate in the United States about these issues.

It is not just when dealing with comatose, severely ill, or obviously terminal patients that the issues related to resuscitation arise. This was not originally a significant concern when the modern era of cardiopulmonary resuscitation began with the discovery that chest compressions or a shock to the heart or both could revive otherwise healthy people who had a sudden cardiac arrest while under anesthesia. As the technology evolved, however, CPR came to be applied widely for many other individuals, ranging from those showing up in emergency rooms without a pulse because of severe trauma and blood loss, to athletes who had a cardiac arrest on the soccer pitch or in the hockey rink. It is not surprising that the outcome of CPR applied in these less controlled situations is less favourable than when the technique is applied within a hospital.

Most hospitals now require complex forms to be completed with respect to resuscitation/end-of-life care plans. While it is highly appropriate to have a clear understanding and agreement with the patient and family about these issues when someone is in imminent danger of dying, such forms have an unfortunate habit of spreading to areas where they are clearly inappropriate. If a teenager overdoses on drugs in a suicide attempt after a failed romance and ends up being critically ill and treated in an intensive care unit because of the need for temporary life support, such a form will likely appear on the chart. Because it is required, a nurse will have to beg the physician to complete it, while recognizing that the patient's (hopefully temporary) wishes are clearly not going to be honoured, nor does the family want them to be.

Equally inappropriate is the routine of asking all patients preoperatively about their wishes with respect to resuscitation. While this may increase the awareness that no operation is completely free of major risk, it is also likely to greatly increase the anxiety of people already anxious about "going under the knife." Furthermore, resuscitation in the very controlled environment of the operating room, where it was first found to be useful, is not only very unlikely to be necessary but also most likely to succeed if it is needed. In spite of this, many patients, worried about being left in a vegetative state after a cardiac arrest, will opt for the DNR box on the preoperative form. A nurse or physician will then have to spend an inordinate amount of time explaining why that is not a good option in this situation. "You don't really mean that, do you?" The default assumption should be that anyone suffering a cardiac arrest in the course of an elective operation should have an attempt at resuscitation. No surgeon relishes the prospect of explaining to the coroner that his patient died in the operating room because of a DNR box carelessly ticked off on a preoperative form.

It is a very different scenario when, as with many severely ill hospitalized individuals, it is very difficult to accurately predict the outcome. In this case, a discussion about the whole spectrum of intensity of treatment becomes very important, and whether or not CPR should be administered in the event of a cardiac arrest is only a minor part of the decision-making. One of the most difficult concepts to get patients and relatives alike to understand is that, in the midst of great uncertainty about the outcome of a severe illness, it may nevertheless be appropriate to *not* undertake certain interventions, such as dialysis or intubation of the trachea for breathing support, while still not giving up and letting the patient die. The frontline caregivers, usually bedside nurses, must sometimes make decisions on short notice when such a patient suddenly deteriorates. In the absence of clear direction from the patient, the medical staff, and the family, they usually and appropriately err on the side of doing more rather than less. But it is in such a situation that clear direction is also often absent, because the patient, the family, or the attending physician, or all three, are uncomfortable in frankly discussing the uncertainties and the futilities of doing things *if*. . . At many Friday rounds, nurses, sensing that someone in their care is likely to crash on the weekend, request but often do not get clear directions about what to do on the weekend *if*. . .

The form used at London Health Sciences Centre to provide direction for frontline caregivers is actually quite clear and explicit, one of only a few of their forms that I can praise for clarity and appropriateness. However, no form ever covers all of the possible developments with such patients, and much is left to the discretion of the nurses. The LHSC form does, however, cover much of the spectrum between full resuscitation and full withdrawal of all support, but interestingly does not include dialysis. Such things as administration of antibiotics, fluids, use of intravenous monitoring, and artificial feeding must be checked off on this form. Often as an attending physician of such patients, I found it was beneficial to address the concerns of the patients, families, and nurses in a two-step process. The first step was to explain, and get the patient's agreement on, the futility of certain interventions in a particular situation, while carefully reassuring her that we were not giving up hope for recovery. The second step, perhaps a day or two later, after the full impact of the first discussion had registered, when the direction of her disease progression had become clearer to everyone, was to explore her wishes about other limitations. Nurses were often thus spared the full force of a tearful, angry patient who felt that she had been completely abandoned to die, which was the result when the full agenda of planned withdrawal of support was presented in one session. A kind of verbal one-two punch, not a TKO in the first round.

The worst situation with a dying patient is when the patient knows that he is dying and everyone around him knows that he is dying, but no one acknowledges it. Eye contact and frank discussion are avoided, and the psychological closure so desperately needed at that point never occurs. In such situations, doctors are often criticized by the nurses for failing to stop useless and sometimes expensive treatments, "pouring money down the drain." At times this is well-deserved criticism, but also at times it is prudent, on a psychological basis, to keep up futile treatments until the patient, or more often the family, have time to adjust to the reality of imminent death. The "Guess what, you are dying," bedside discussion was never one of my favourite tasks, but it was common to come to this with great trepidation, only to find that the patient was far ahead of everyone else, including the family and the health-care team, in sensing what was transpiring. It was often a relief to the patient to find that others finally recognized the reality that he had already accepted.

Fear of becoming a brain-damaged dependent as a result of attempts to be resuscitated from a cardiac arrest is one of the often-cited reasons for patients to request a DNR status when they are not even critically ill and have good prospects for full recovery from an acute illness or injury. Widely publicized cases, such as that of Terri Schiavo, intensify such fears, but are relatively uncommon—at least relative to the usual reasons for developing crippling and dehumanizing brain dysfunction. Slowly developing dementias, such as Alzheimer's, are much more common causes of an existence resembling that of Terri Schiavo's vegetative state, without meaningful communication of any kind. It is paradoxical that we frequently consider such a state of existence as a fate worse than death for ourselves, and would request a DNR status on the basis of that possibility, yet rail at those who may consider it appropriate to take irreversible brain dysfunction into account when making decisions about the intensity of care applied to others. The furor and hyperbole about the Obama health-care reform of 2010 leading to withdrawing care for Grandma in the locked ward of a dingy nursing home illustrate this inconsistency.

Most of the right-wing alarmists who used this fear-mongering to oppose the reforms because they would lead to killing off the old and infirm would probably, when considering their own options, choose a DNR status rather than any possibility of being maintained in a vegetative state themselves. Yet they insist that this is an appropriate state for their loved ones to be maintained in.

The Terri Schiavo case is instructive in many ways other than for the involvement of the judicial, legislative, and executive branches of the United States government in the end-of-life debate. First, the cardiac arrest that resulted in her persistent vegetative state occurred at home, at a young age, likely as a complication of a longstanding eating disorder. The possibility of resuscitation from an out-of-hospital cardiac arrest has led to huge and expensive programs to train lay people in the technique of CPR, and to the installation of defibrillators in many public buildings and institutions such as sports facilities. However, successful resuscitation of these individuals is unusual, and those who do recover heart function are very likely to die in hospital later during the next days or months. Those whose bodies do survive are, like Terri Schiavo, likely to have significant brain damage. This is in stark contrast to resuscitation in the controlled environment of a hospital, or, better still, in an operating room. In one Ontario study,[1] reported in the *New England Journal of Medicine*, of the effectiveness of advanced cardiac life support administered by paramedics at the scene of an out-of-hospital arrest, a situation likely to be associated with better outcomes than if the resuscitation is administered by bystanders with minimal training, only 3 percent of all the subjects survived to hospital discharge even if their heart had been restarted successfully. Twenty-nine percent of that 3 percent had some significant cognitive impairment. A 2-percent chance of surviving intact may alternatively be considered better than no chance or worse than dying, if it carries with it a high risk of leading a poor quality of life for only a short period of time thereafter, and then dying. The study only tracked survival to discharge from hospital, and was designed to test the validity of criteria to stop resuscitation because of futility.

Second, the Schiavo case illustrates the problems that arise when longstanding family feuds spill over into the decision-making with respect to end-of-life care. When careful and repeated discussion by the health-care team with the patient and/or next-of-kin or power-of-attorney fails to result in a plan of care that everyone can agree upon, it is sometimes because the doctors or nurses fail to describe the situation accurately. However, it is more often because one or more members of the family bring preconceived ideas and distrust to the table—either distrust of the motives of the health-care team or of the other members of the family. It is in such situations that ethics committees, lawyers, and even politicians get involved. Such was clearly the case in the escalation of the dispute over what to do about Terri Schiavo's feeding tube.

Third, the Schiavo case is a typical although extreme example of what happens in DNR / end-of-life decisions when there is no clearly defined and uncontested decision-making authority assigned to one individual, either by a living will or by law. She had no living will at the time of her cardiac arrest. Her husband, with possibly some monetary as well as compassionate motives for wanting to let her die, and her parents, with rigid Roman Catholic beliefs about not facilitating her exit to what they professed to believe would be a better existence, fought over who should have the power to decide whether or not to remove her feeding tube. When lawyers, public defenders, courts, and politicians got involved, the rhetoric was ratcheted up to a national level, facts were obscured in hyperbole, and millions of dollars of taxpayers' money was spent without any benefit to the unfortunate patient. Perhaps the only good to come out of this was the reminder to everyone to be very clear about his/her own wishes in such a circumstance, to have in writing a living will and a designated power of attorney that no real attorney can dispute, and to discuss these issues with those designated individuals. Should completion of a living will be mandated by law, just as is filing an income tax return?

Fourth and last, few situations involving end-of-life decisions are free of religious influences, and these played a prominent role in the Schiavo case. It is, of course, highly appropriate to be aware of the patient's religious beliefs when discussing plans to designate a DNR status or to withdraw support for a patient who is about to die. It is also appropriate for the nurse or physician to question how his own beliefs may influence the conversations. Although I have never heard a nurse ask a dying patient to give her regards to her favourite uncle when the patient gets to the next world, there is no doubt that the caregiver's beliefs about an afterlife influence what they say to a dying patient. It always seems odd to me that those, whether patients, physicians, nurses, or policymakers, who most firmly profess to believe that they are going to go to a better place to be reunited with their loved ones, are also the most likely to refuse any intervention that might smooth the road or hasten their journey to that place. They also want to deny others any such interventions as a matter of public policy, forcing their belief in the "sanctity of life" on those of us who admit that we do not fully understand what that term means. They seem to see no conflict, however, in advocating for capital punishment to speed the delivery of felons into what they believe will be an unending life of torture in hell. The paradox of atheists being comfortable with assisted suicide for themselves in spite of believing that there is simply nothingness thereafter, while the most pious religious believers tenaciously cling to a miserable life here, even though they believe there is a better one in store for them, is discussed at length by Sir Richard Dawkins.[2]

A close friend recently commented to me that, although he did not hold any specific religious beliefs, he would have no objection to having a priest present at his dying moment, just in case they had it right and he was all wrong—what have you got to lose at that point? If there is a next life, my own position is that I am prepared to be surprised, but I don't expect anything. To quote Voltaire: "Doubt is not a pleasant condition, but certainty is absurd." I have also vowed to never do anything in this life just because I might be rewarded for it in the next one, a position that was reinforced by the events of 9/11. The extreme expression of ultimate selfishness is to suicide bomb people here because you believe that will earn you the companionship of seventy-two voluptuous virgins waiting for you in the next world. This belief raises problems for those of us who may share the fantasy but not the belief. When we have to deal with such women when they are desperately ill here, should we encourage them to tick off the DNR box to ensure that the supply in the next world does not become depleted? With the recent increase in suicide bombings, are they now back-ordered? Although suicide acts done for rewards in the next life are extreme, lesser acts of either good or evil done solely for the rewards you believe are waiting for you in heaven are fundamentally in the same motivational category—expressions of selfishness, albeit with a more admirable capacity for delayed gratification.

No discussion of end-of-life issues is complete without including some consideration of suicide. This was a criminal act until the Canadian Criminal Code was modified in 1972, although it is hard to see how even the most determined judge could convict someone who did it successfully. Only those who failed even at this last desperate act could actually be punished for trying and failing. Suicide is in one sense a very selfish act, depriving those left behind of a proper farewell and leaving them with a lot of guilt about how they could have seen it coming and perhaps prevented it. A certain stigma attached to it spills over onto the family and friends—unless the person is rich and famous or notorious and infamous, in which case we may grant some grudging admiration for the individual who had the courage to end it all. Suicide does not seem to have diminished the admiration for or popularity of Socrates, Brutus, Hannibal, Ernest Hemingway, Virginia Woolf, Kurt Cobain, or even Heath Ledger. The suicide of John P. Robarts did not diminish the esteem for him represented in the famous local Robarts Research Institute at the University of Western Ontario, the Centre for Canadian Studies named after him at York University, the library named after him at the University of Toronto, and the two schools named after him in London. Even the suicide of Miss Proper, Amy Vanderbilt, did not seem to render her advice about etiquette any the less relevant. Our attitudes about suicide seem to be related to how far we are from the individual on the social distance scale (see Chapter 7)—it is okay for Not Our Sort of People (NOSPs) and celebrities who are far removed from us to commit suicide when they have come to regard life here as unbearable. It is not approved for ordinary folk who are closer to us on that scale; they must be made to suffer interminable misery in the twilight before being allowed to die.

Most suicides in physically healthy people, however, are the result of mental illnesses that are usually very treatable, and it is truly a tragedy when such an illness is not recognized or adequately treated and results in an unnecessary death. But to extend an enforced prevention strategy from this scenario to someone who is dying a slow, painful death seems to me to be cruel. After all, we do let people kill themselves slowly all the time, provided they do so using the principles of freedom and autonomy in proscribed ways, and provided the moment of death is not as predictable as with a gunshot or a drug overdose. We let people with alcoholic liver disease continue to drink, we let diabetics refuse to take insulin, and we even let dialysis-dependent kidney patients refuse further dialysis. If you can successfully persuade your nephrologist that you are sane (whatever that means) and that you understand the fatal consequences of stopping dialysis, that decision cannot be appealed to an ethics committee or a court, and you may get your wish to die.

Most experienced nurses and physicians of my acquaintance who have watched many people die will admit that the line between ensuring comfort for a dying patient and hastening their death is a blurred one at best. They have no qualms about giving the last dose of a potent narcotic to someone who is in obvious distress, even if the patient stops breathing within minutes because of the effects of that dose. While we can't admit that we hasten death, lest we be charged with murder, the truth is that we all know that we do, and we also know that we ourselves would never want to suffer in the way we sometimes make our patients suffer in their last days of life on earth. Most of my physician acquaintances who talk about this honestly express the hope that there will be someone able and willing to help them give that fatal dose of narcotic if or when they are obviously terminally ill; at least one that I know has a supply of an intravenous general anesthetic stored away for just such an occasion.

I would like to have it on the record that if I were to experience (suffer is too harsh a term for such a painless quick exit) a cardiac arrest at home, at the curling rink, or out on the bike path, I hope that some bystander or paramedic would succeed in restarting my heart so that my body could arrive at a hospital emergency room with it beating. Given the data about the low probability of having a functioning brain at that point, I would also hope to not have any brain left functioning, thereby avoiding the possibility of being kept alive in a dependent vegetative state. I hope that my body would then fulfill the criteria for brain death. The person that I currently am would, in this scenario, have long since departed to the next world, if there is one. If this wish were granted, someone else with a real prospect of a real life could hopefully benefit from the use of any number of organs that were once in my possession, by their removal for transplantation. The possibility of this benefit to others, not even mentioned in studies of out-of-hospital resuscitation, seems to me to be the major reason to continue such efforts.

Notes

1. L.J. Morrison, L.M. Visentin, A. Kiss, R. Therialt, et al., "Validation of a Rule for the Termination of Resuscitation in Out-of-Hospital Cardiac Arrest," *New England Journal of Medicine* 353 (2006): 478–87.
2. Richard Dawkins, *The God Delusion* (New York: Bantam Books, 2006).

10

Ethics Committees

The morality of morality cops

Self-righteous indignation, or at best an admission of poor judgment, is likely to be your response—at least your public response—to any suggestion that your behaviour has been unethical. This is equally true whether you are a politician, businessman, professional sportsman, cleric, or health-care worker. Nevertheless, we all know that unethical behaviour pervades all these fields, and that there are serious consequences. In each of these areas, there are now "watchdog" organizations, in some cases several layers of them, both within organizations and external to them, to monitor the behaviour of the workers and to deal with complaints about unethical practices.

In the field of health care, the watchdogs are usually the professional licensing bodies of the various professions, the institutional review boards of universities and research institutes, and the internal ethics committees of hospitals. For the price of a stamp and a sheet of paper, anyone can start a formal complaint against a doctor, nurse, or other health-care practitioner by sending a letter of complaint to the appropriate college. For research, whether it is a simple questionnaire sent to a random sample of a particular population, or a proposal to do a sham operation in a controlled trial of a surgical procedure, the approval of an institutional review board is a prerequisite if the researcher is affiliated with an institution. Similar approval is not required for a political party, a polling firm, or a media outlet to research the opinions of a particular population.

However, much of the monitoring of the moral behaviour of practitioners is left to fellow practitioners who on a day-to-day basis provide some pressure to conform to normal ethical practices.

At times, that peer monitoring is a binding obligation: For instance, a physician who becomes aware of an allegation of sexual abuse of a patient by a fellow physician is obliged to report the allegation to the college or risk discipline himself if he does not do so. And anyone directly involved in the care of a hospital inpatient can request a consultation with an ethicist, although this is commonly done only as a team after discussions fail to resolve a difficult ethical issue such as the possible withdrawal of care from a terminally ill patient when the patient and/or family cannot agree on a proper course of action.

Institutional review boards for research are often accused by researchers of being slow, cumbersome, and obsessed with grammar and minutiae. The less-flattering adjective I hear most often from my peers is "picky." I would add that they are inconsistent as well. The last research project I participated in that required such approval asked participants with a particular disease to fill out a ten-minute questionnaire, have a brief examination that was required for their care anyway, and submit a blood sample for analysis. Granted, this sample was to be tested on a genome-wide basis for genes that we hoped to find were associated with their disease, and genetic testing is a sensitive issue with all sorts of privacy implications. The Institutional Review Board at the University of Toronto had approved the application for patients of a colleague there before I became an additional investigator in the study. Nevertheless, when I submitted the same research protocol with the exact same wording of the consent form to the Institutional Review Board at the University of Western Ontario, using the forms designed by them, they refused to approve it until I had made more than fifty changes to the wording, mainly to the consent form. After making many changes, the reviewers of the revisions requested further revisions, with some of the suggested wording reverting back to what I had originally submitted. Is the ethical treatment of research subjects that much different between Toronto and London that those completely different forms must be used to get the approval?

Many researchers are concerned that the process of obtaining institutional review board approval for studies is so slow and cumbersome in some places that it affects academic careers. Individual researchers in institutions that perform this function quickly and efficiently are being favoured over those in other places. This is true for multi-centre and particularly international studies where competitive enrollment is the norm. By this I mean that once an industry sponsor has developed a study, perhaps to evaluate a new drug, they invite researchers at various sites to become the investigators. The centres that can get their institutional review board approval for participation quickly are likely to have more subjects enrolled by the enrolment deadline than are those with a slower approval process. Getting the maximum number of subjects enrolled in a study has major implications not only for financial compensation to individuals and institutions, but also to academic credentials. The individual with the record of highest enrollment in a study is likely to be the lead author of the scientific research paper reporting the results. This has nothing to do with the diligence or ethical principles of a researcher. For so-called investigator-initiated studies, similar concerns apply. Your academic physician may have a brilliant hypothesis that a new application of an old treatment will lead to a major breakthrough in the treatment of your miserable disease or symptoms. Quite apart from being able to find the funds to do the study, if she cannot get institutional review board approval at enough sites to enroll enough patients to test the hypothesis scientifically, the brilliance will be wasted, and the hypothesis will never be tested.

I participated in one further research project that presented a completely different process. This was an industry-sponsored international study evaluating a new laboratory test. The study was not based in any academic facility. My participation as the Canadian principal investigator and that of my co-investigators was not directly related to any hospital or university. The ethics review board that approved it was also not part of any academic centre, but rather a private group of health-care professionals. The application and consent forms were all submitted by the industrial sponsor on our behalf. I am uncertain about the financial or other relationships between the institutional review board and the sponsor of the study (I don't want to know), but the process was certainly much easier from the researcher's viewpoint, and consistent for all seventeen Canadian sites participating in the study.

The approval of revisions of the protocol and the submission of various bits of information and progress reports was also handled by the sponsor, although the amount of time spent on checking various electronic forms for accuracy and auditing those forms still seemed excessive for such a simple study.

It is certainly true that industry-sponsored trials should be monitored and reviewed to protect research subjects and to ensure scientific integrity. A pharmaceutical company is unlikely to sponsor a study comparing its drug with that of its competitor without some hope that their product will show superior results. They are prone to building that assurance of superiority into the design of the study or to use some complicated statistical manipulations to convince the reader of the study results that their product really is superior. The worst of them may try to prohibit publication of the results by the investigators without the company's permission if the results do not favour their product. This unethical practice has become much more difficult, since all reputable observational or interventional clinical trials conducted in North America are now registered with ClinicalTrials.gov, a database maintained by the United States National Institutes of Health. This database now contains information on more than 90,000 such trials. Any local institutional review board requires any industry-sponsored trial protocol to be registered at this site, a very useful safeguard to at least ensure transparency.

Health Canada also monitors the pharmaceutical research companies' internal monitors and does random audits and site visits to the investigators to review the documentation in so-called source documents (participants' clinical records). Furthermore, any scientist that reports results of a clinical trial in any reputable scientific journal must disclose any financial or other conflict of interest that might influence the conclusions. On the flip side, a claim that accompanies the health food store concoction to cleanse your liver or ease your depression may cite a controlled trial showing that it works. If that study is not registered at ClinicalTrials.gov and the trial researchers do not disclose their relationship to the manufacturer, such claims should be viewed with great skepticism.

Institutional review boards are less consistently involved in oversight of retrospective case series reports, individual case reports of unusual problems, and correlation studies, all of which are also generally less scientifically conclusive. They are, however, a favourite topic for the medical media and advertisers. The fact that there is an overall *correlation* between sun exposure and skin cancer, for example, a favourite warning in common advertisements on the weather channels everywhere, does not prove a cause and effect relationship, but it is widely accepted that sun exposure causes skin cancer. But if this is so, why does malignant melanoma, the only commonly lethal form of skin cancer, usually occur in sites that are often not exposed to the sun at all? No company that produces sunscreen products is likely to submit an application to an ethics review board to do a proper controlled trial of their product in preventing this deadly disease. It might well reduce their sales.

In the area of disagreements about what should be done where there is a genuine ethical dilemma in an inpatient setting, inclusion of an ethicist or an ethics committee can go a long way toward resolving the conflict, but they seldom provide definitive advice. As an ethicist who was involved in the decision-making with one of my patients pointed out to me, he saw his job on the team as simply asking relevant questions that no one else had considered, rather than providing answers to those questions. It has always seemed peculiar to me that although ethicists are quite willing to ask questions about balancing the best interests of the individual patient with those of society at large, they are unwilling to tackle a similar balancing act when the question is one of hospital policy. What are the relative ethical merits of closing an operating room for a few days to help in balancing the hospital budget compared to some other cuts that could be undertaken to accomplish the same thing? No one will get input on that from the hospital ethicist.

Hospital ethics committees can be not only helpful, but can be critical in formulating an appropriate policy for the hospital. To cite one personal example, in the early days of liver transplantation at what was then University Hospital in London, Ontario, the liver transplant team faced a dilemma we could not solve. We knew from experience and from the literature that we could successfully save the lives of alcoholics dying from alcoholic liver disease—they usually fared as well as others undergoing the procedure for diseases unrelated to lifestyle, at least in the short term. However, because of the shortage of donors, the effect of doing this on everyone needing it would be that some people on the waiting list, with disease that their behaviour had not caused, would die while awaiting a donor liver. The obligation of a physician when dealing with an individual patient, enshrined in the Hippocratic Oath, is that we should consider only the best interests of the patient, but we felt an obligation as well to use the scarce resource of donated livers in a way that was also in the best interests of society as a whole. We were concerned, for example, that indiscriminate use of this resource might decrease the rate of organ donation; relatives of brain-dead potential donors might be less willing to consent to organ donation if they believed that the organ might save the life of someone such as a skid-row alcoholic dying of liver failure. A telephone survey we did actually supported this concern. We also had legitimate criticism of the selection process for liver transplantation voiced at least occasionally by intensive care nurses, the very people most likely to identify potential donors and initiate the discussion of possible organ donation with their relatives. The optics became as important as the survival data.

We took these concerns about conflicting obligations to the hospital ethics committee. Although it was a long process and they asked for more meetings to clarify the issues, the final result was nothing short of brilliant. Recognizing that no one is perfect, they considered that the cause of the disease should not be a prohibitive factor in deciding on its treatment. Nevertheless, the care after liver transplantation does require adherence to a fairly strict regimen of taking medication and attending follow-up checks; otherwise the resource investment is likely to be wasted and the patient is likely to die. Accordingly, they adopted a simple one-sentence policy statement to the effect that: "Everyone coming for liver transplantation assessment must demonstrate to the team's satisfaction that they are able to comply with reasonable medical advice." Full stop. This became official hospital policy.

For the transplant team, that meant that we had to carefully assess compliance (the politically correct term has now changed to *adherence* for some mysterious reason) in each individual. For someone with alcoholic liver disease, "reasonable medical advice" is to completely abstain from alcohol use. We chose to require this for a minimum of six months, outside of hospital, before being listed, with careful assessment of their commitment to continue this by the transplant social worker and sometimes by an addictions specialist. We also were obliged to consider adherence in other aspects, such as taking medication and adhering to the restricted diet that is often a necessary part of their treatment regimen. The emphasis was rightly switched from the cause of the disease to the ability of the patient to look after himself. We could then tell a patient with alcoholic liver disease that we could offer transplantation, but would be prohibited from doing so by hospital policy unless she demonstrated an ability to abstain from alcohol and to adhere to the routine of care. We then presented this policy to the Canadian Liver Transplant Study Group, which adopted the same policy for implementation at all the other Canadian liver transplant centres that were starting to struggle with the same issue.

Not all ethicists have been so helpful to medical practitioners and some have been quite annoying in spouting opinions without bothering with facts. A student from the Westminster Institute for Ethics and Human Values (a University of Western Ontario think tank) published an article in their newsletter that was very critical of our acceptance of a patient with alcoholic liver disease for transplantation, after being allowed to attend our weekly selection conference as a student/guest. Not only were the facts of the case misrepresented (ethicists and philosophers will point out that facts are all about perceptions), but the patient could easily be identified in the newsletter article, a clear breach of patient confidentiality. There is only one mayor of most towns, and the town was named, as well as the fact that he was the sitting mayor. Who disciplines unethical behaviour by ethicists? We did extract an apology to the team and the patient in this situation.

The life of an ethicist must be difficult. When you are the morality cop, how do you deal with your own moral failings and the expectations of others that you should have none? We accept that lawmakers often break the law, clergy often don't believe what they preach, and doctors often fail to look after their own health. Worse still, some investment bankers sometimes rob their customers, some police sometimes act like street thugs, some priests sometimes abuse their altar boys, and some doctors sometimes tailor their practices to maximize their income, or sexually abuse their patients. But it is not a pretty picture of our society that we see if we come to believe that all of us need watchdogs to keep us honest and moral, as the daily reporting of human failures might make us believe. If the emphasis of the popular media is any indication of the public's appetite, we must all get an ego boost from discovering that those apparently perfect people a long way from us on the social distance scale actually have weaknesses and character defects, and that they yield to temptations that we have experienced but resisted. And we should accept that ethicists sometimes behave unethically themselves, and that most of us behave ethically—most of the time.

In contrast, the starting point in the proliferation of ethics watchdog organizations seems to be the assumption that everyone acts unethically most of the time until proven otherwise. If this is truly the case, we need divine help, not the help of another flawed human being. Adding a committee of ethicists to every organization, including every public hospital and university, will not solve the problem, any more than adding an ethics watchdog to a political system will suddenly make politicians keep their promises. But it certainly provides great employment opportunities for individuals with a doctorate in moral philosophy whose job prospects are otherwise rather slim.

11

Protocols

The risks of routines

My eighteen-year-old son arrived in the emergency room with some obvious minor injuries after a collision with a car while on his bicycle. The trauma protocol indicated that he should be kept NPO (nothing by mouth) in case he was found to have some internal injuries and might need an operation to remove a ruptured spleen. He got progressively worse over a few hours of observation: His blood pressure dropped and he got lightheaded each time they tried to stand him up, worsening the fears that he had some internal bleeding. No one questioned the circumstances of the accident, or his routine—that was not in the protocol. The collision had occurred close to the end of his regular twenty-four-kilometre bike trip home on a hot summer day. His routine was to arrive home a bit dehydrated and immediately consume at least two litres of fluids. Several hours later, when I got the message about the accident, with the alarming news that his vital signs were unstable, I arrived in the emergency room, fortunately without a speeding ticket, to find him well but frustrated at being kept there. I surreptitiously turned up the rate of the intravenous fluids from the "To keep the vein open" rate (as per the trauma protocol) and found that after a few litres of fluid he was able to stand up without dropping his blood pressure. I was lectured about interfering, but at least got him out of the ER without further unnecessary investigations or an unnecessary operation.

This example illustrates just one of the problems in following a routine without thinking of the consequences. I am sure that readers will be able to relate many similar stories where blindly following the protocol led to ignoring an individual's unique circumstances.

The use of protocols and preprinted order forms is perhaps one of the fastest areas of growth in all of medicine. I am basing most of the discussion that follows on those that are readily available on-line at the LHSC Web site,[1] although there are undoubtedly hundreds of others in use in many other institutions. At last count, there are no fewer than twenty-one of these developed specifically for use in the Critical Care Trauma Unit at London Health Sciences Centre. This does not include many that are in widespread use in other areas of the same hospital that may well find their way onto the chart of a patient in any area of the institution. There are special pages of preprinted orders for almost every aspect of care in every area of the hospital, ranging from post-operative prophylaxis of blood clotting after orthopedic surgery to a full page of routine investigations and consultation requests for a seriously ill patient being assessed for possible liver transplantation.

Why the proliferation of these forms? In the 1970s, the only acronym I had to remember when admitting a patient was DAB SPIT. This was designed to remind me that I should always write something on the first page of orders about Diet, Activity (bed rest, bathroom only, etc.), Bowels (don't forget to order a laxative as needed), Sedative, Procedures, Investigations, and Treatment. Failing to remember any one of these components could mean a sleepless night as an irritated nurse might call you frequently to write the order for any of them that you had omitted, often one at a time several times through the night. With the increasing complexity of care and specialization, however, this little acronym clearly does not now cover the gamut of necessary investigations, procedures, and treatments, and many of these components of routine care are now incorporated into some form of protocol, or preprinted order form.

There are many benefits to using these forms. The first is sheer convenience and clarity. If an ordering physician simply has to check off the appropriate option on a preprinted electrolyte replacement menu, for example, the result is likely to at least be legible and less dangerous than an illegible handwritten order. When dealing with a severely ill liver patient who may or may not need or qualify for liver transplantation, the input of multiple specialists and many investigations are required to come up with the right decision; this is most easily assured by using a preprinted order form to get the consultations and investigations done expeditiously. If, a few days later, the surgeon has spent sixteen or more hours in the operating room with the donor retrieval and then doing the transplant on that same liver patient, he is likely to appreciate a preprinted order form for post-operative care, including the anti-rejection drugs needed, the routine of diet, and the frequency of blood and urine testing, rather than having to think through the individual components of DAB SPIT.

Second, the explosion of reliable scientific evidence indicating that certain routines improve the outcomes in carefully defined situations, usually with a very specific population of patients, make it ethically questionable to continue the practice of having one routine for Dr. X's post-operative care and a completely different routine for the same patient population of Dr. Y if one or both of those routines differ substantially from the evidence-based standard. Preprinted orders ensure some consistency and adherence to guidelines and best practices. There is solid evidence, for example, that the majority of patients after a coronary artery bypass grafting have better chances of a smooth recovery and longer survival by following a routine of several medications. Similarly, radiologists obtain the best possible CT scan or MRI images of the abdomen if they use a standard predetermined protocol for patient fasting and for administration and timing of an injection of contrast material.

Third, protocols and preprinted orders can be a very useful teaching tool in academic centres, provided they are used appropriately. The resident who carefully studies and understands the rationale for a preprinted insulin regimen for critically ill patients may be educated about its importance, and may even be able to use something similar in other settings, perhaps outside the teaching hospital. Preprinted orders for monitoring nutritional status may send a subtle message to everyone about the importance of involving nutritionists in the routine care of many patients, something that is frequently neglected in teaching hospitals.

Fourth, preprinted orders are likely to reduce errors, whether of medication or of neglect. A pharmacist on a committee to develop such protocols is likely to spot potentially serious drug interactions before the patient gets the medication in question. A form for weaning a patient off narcotic painkillers is likely to prevent both too rapid weaning, leading to withdrawal symptoms, and too slow weaning, leading to a risk of overdosing and even longer-term dependence or addiction. A preprinted order form dictating a chest x-ray before nutritional supplements are delivered into a newly placed feeding tube ensures that no supplement is inadvertently poured into some patient's trachea. This also, however, frequently requires a special trip back to the hospital on the weekend to view the x-ray, unless it can be viewed at home via the electronic record.

Some protocols are not as clearly beneficial as the examples above. A three-page, complicated, preprinted order form for induction of mild hypothermia after cardiac arrest is available; although the procedure may improve the chances of preserving brain function, this is not yet well documented in controlled trials, and the risks of hypothermia are substantial, especially when many other things are being done to the patient at the same time. It also requires a very labour-intensive monitoring routine. Another protocol dictates that no patient can receive recombinant Factor VII (a blood product used sparingly but with benefit to a few patients with severe infections) without review by a hematologist; this may be an appropriate precaution for safety, although one could question whether or not it is simply reducing costs to the pharmacy budget and increasing revenue to the hematologist.

Although the use of routines, preprinted orders, and protocols is undoubtedly useful in every area of modern hospital practice—and even office practice—there are some obvious concerns and even dangers. First is the none-too-subtle message that we can all be treated the same when we are ill and in a health-care facility—as illustrated by the experience of my son with the trauma protocol. The implication is that the health-care team does not need to know anything about the person, just about the disease, procedure, or operation. This may be true in veterinary medicine and in field hospitals in war zones, but it is not true in most hospitals that claim to offer "patient-centred care."

Second, following preprinted orders commonly leads to unnecessary investigation and treatment. The investigative protocol referred to above for "workup" of a potential liver transplant candidate includes tests for most of the common and some rare forms of liver disease, even though in the vast majority of individuals the diagnosis has been firmly established by that time and the tests have already been done, often outside the transplant centre. The patient listed for transplantation who is fortunate enough to get a donated liver within a few days of listing will then have many of the same tests and at least a chest x-ray repeated on the day of the surgery, as there is a separate set of preprinted orders for investigation immediately prior to the operation. Similar duplications of testing and procedures undoubtedly exist in many other fields of medicine. It is easier to follow protocols blindly than to think through the rationale of what is really needed for individual circumstances and make deliberate exceptions. I frequently received telephoned or faxed requests to consult on a patient that I had admitted, simply because "Consult Dr. Ghent" was on the preprinted orders for a pre-transplant assessment–a harmless waste of time, but a waste nevertheless.

Third, slapping a set of preprinted orders onto a chart without considering the circumstances can lead to significant confusion and contradictions. In perusing an intensive care unit chart recently, I noted that it included eleven pages of such orders with at least five orders that were incompatible with each other. What is a bedside nurse to do when the surgeon checks off a set of analgesia orders on a post-coronary artery bypass form, and an intensivist checks off a different routine set of analgesia orders for the same patient on a separate form used only in the intensive care unit? These discrepancies may extend to the frequency of blood testing, of monitoring various functions, and the type or rate of infusions of fluids.

Fourth, and last, extensive use of protocols and routines probably has a negative overall impact on the teaching of trainees. Unless a resident deliberately takes the time to review every set of preprinted orders she ever signs, and makes a point of understanding the reason for each checkbox on it, the form is likely to be a substitute for thinking about what is needed rather than a stimulus to do any thinking, whereas teaching should be all about thinking–and thinking critically. If she does think critically, there may well be some uncomfortable questions directed at the experts who develop these forms; "because that is the way we do it" is not a good enough answer. One of the protocols still in use[2] includes giving "KCl bolus I.V.," KCl being potassium chloride, and bolus widely understood to mean delivery of a relatively large amount of medication quickly. This form, however, refers to another form that advises that the KCl must be given as a slow infusion, by definition *not* a bolus. Giving an intravenous bolus of KCl is how many U.S. states carry out executions, and in the hospital setting, delivering an ordered fatal bolus of KCl has led to several legitimate malpractice suits against doctors, nurses, and hospitals. No one seems to have recognized that combining "bolus" and "KCl" in the same sentence is not the best way to teach trainees how to treat a low potassium level safely, which suggests that no one has critically read the protocol at all.

In a similar vein, years ago, with much internal fanfare, the Forms Committee at London Health Sciences Centre announced that they had developed a new Death Package. This was supposedly going to make it easier for house staff, nurses, and other staff to follow a standard routine and get all the paperwork done properly and expeditiously when a patient died. While not strictly a protocol, it included the difficult-to-follow instruction that "the patient shall sign the Consent to Autopsy Form" as part of the routine. This seems to be taking patient-centred care a little too far. Did anyone actually read this before distributing it to every ward? I am not sure if this form is still in use or has even been read by the front-line workers.

I have never served on a forms committee and I am sure no hospital administrator would ever want me to. However, from the perspective of an outside practitioner who had to deal with hospital forms frequently, it seems to me that some simple guidelines, if implemented, would improve the effectiveness of many protocols and preprinted forms.

First, no preprinted orders should ever be approved by a forms committee unless and until they have been critically reviewed by a group of end users, not just from the specialty involved, but from other areas that may frequently interact with the specialty. The radiologists should be involved, for example, if the protocol involves any x-rays, and a pharmacist with any that involves administration of any medication, especially, perhaps, those dangerous non-prescription ones like aspirin. This is not just to ensure safety, but also to ensure value. And the accounting office penny-pinchers should be specifically excluded–it is too easy to end up with a second-rate generic medication if the cost of one part of the care is considered in isolation.

For example, dabigatran etaxilate is a new orally administered blood thinner that is at least as effective and safe as heparin or coumadin in preventing post-operative blood clotting. It is also much more expensive than either heparin or coumadin, if pharmacy budget costs are considered alone. However, its use does not require any needles, syringes, blood sampling for monitoring, laboratory testing, or dosage adjustments. A front office pharmacy manager will no doubt complain about the cost to his department of switching to dabigatran, which may be of considerable benefit and convenience to everyone else, including the patient, and its use may lower the costs in other areas of the hospital. The total cost to the institution may therefore be no higher than for heparin or coumadin.

On the flip side, there should be some mechanism to ensure that protocols are not designed with maximizing the income for their developers in mind. Should there be a "consumer" representative, i.e., a patient, on the forms committee to guard against using protocols for such self-serving purposes?

Second, there should be an expiry or mandatory revision date on all preprinted orders. As new evidence of benefit arrives from reliable scientific studies, it is just good clinical practice to incorporate these into any protocols; the easiest way to ensure that this happens is to set a funeral date for all forms at the time of their birth. This would be most easily accomplished if all of the orders and options were in an electronic format, thereby eliminating the problem of stocking dozens of pigeon holes in dozens of wards with paper forms that live on long past their usefulness and may accidentally find their way onto a chart.

Third, flexibility needs to be a guiding principle of all preprinted orders. A blood glucose monitoring and treatment protocol, to be at all useful, must be able to accommodate the unique circumstances of the individual. A severely stressed diabetic recovering from a pancreas transplant should probably not be given insulin to keep the blood sugars in the same narrow range that would be appropriate for other stressed surgical patients, and someone on a tapering regimen of steroids is likely to have severely and dangerously low blood sugars if blindly given insulin as per a rigid protocol. The patient just back from the operating room who has just been found to have a terminal cancer and who has no hope of rehabilitation should not be expected to go through the same rigorous post-operative physiotherapy rehabilitation routine as someone who has just had his cancer totally removed. The investigations and monitoring routines in protocols also need to be flexible enough to avoid the frequent over-investigation that is a real danger of following protocols. For example, the protocol for CT scanning of the abdomen requires fasting to get the best images. However, if the patient has no gallbladder and the specific question being asked is whether or not the mass in the liver is an abscess, fasting is really not necessary; following the protocol that requires it will only delay the investigation and contribute to the malnutrition that is so common in hospitalized patients unnecessarily kept fasting for various tests.

Finally, to be useful for teaching purposes, all preprinted orders and protocols need to be systematically studied and explained to everyone using them. If the trainee asks why the recently inserted stomach feeding tube position needs to be checked with an x-ray before feeding is begun, and no one has a good answer, that part of the protocol for feeding tube placement should be deleted from the protocol. It was once good enough to listen to the abdomen with a stethoscope while injecting some air into the tube and listening for the bubbling that indicates that the tube is in the stomach and not in the trachea. But that assumes there is someone at the bedside and that that someone actually has a stethoscope. Those are big assumptions.

Investigative and treatment protocols and all kinds of other routines are here to stay in all health-care institutions. From a patient's viewpoint, it is appropriate to inquire whether the testing and treatment you are receiving is because you need it or merely because it is in the protocol. Since I no longer have any hospital privileges, my hope is that the only hospital form anyone needs to use on me is that Death Package, and that the staff do not expect me to sign the Consent for Autopsy Form.

Notes

1. London Health Sciences Centre. http://www.lhsc.on.ca/Health_Professionals/CCTC/protocols/index.htm. Accessed July 9, 2010.

2. "Continuous Renal Replacement Therapy Preprinted Orders" (heparin or no anticoagulation) in above site. Found at the Web site: http://www.lhsc.on.ca/Health_Professionals/CCTC/protocols/2009_basic_crrt.pdf. Accessed July 9, 2010.

℞ 12

Treating Numbers

Easier than treating patients

A recent radio program I happened to be listening to featured an interview with a urologist, discussing the miracles that can be achieved by using supplements to treat low testosterone levels in middle-aged and elderly men. He said that this not only increases their libido and their sexual performance, it also increases their muscle mass, staves off depression, improves their cognitive powers, and prevents the development of Alzheimer's disease. It does not prevent the tendency for its proponents to claim to have found the fountain of youth, which has been a staple of charlatans for centuries. A recent series of articles in the *New England Journal of Medicine*[1,2,3] provides a more balanced perspective. Although the term "late-onset hypogonadism" seems to imply that there is a real disease that is common and treatable in older men, an accompanying research paper concludes that treatment with supplemental testosterone may be worse than the "disease."

The above debate is one of many examples of modern medicine's tendency to treat numbers rather than the patient. One of the problems this creates, as illustrated in this case, is the difficulty of determining what can be considered "normal." If half of all men over a certain age have blood testosterone levels that are below normal, but those levels correlate poorly or not at all with any significant symptoms, perhaps what needs to be changed is the definition of normal, not the blood levels.

None of us is likely to be found to be completely normal, medically or otherwise, if we are tested in enough ways. A psychiatrist encountering this cynical, opinionated, retired hepatologist who, with no previous non-academic published works, aims to publish a book of essays on modern medicine for the general public, may well determine that I am not normal, without ever seeing me. (They appear to have no hesitation in diagnosing psychiatric diseases without seeing the patient, as evidenced by the volumes written about the psychiatric illnesses of historical figures.) I have no intention of letting any psychiatrist analyze me, but any number of labels might be applied: narcissistic personality disorder or perhaps a delusional disorder, with delusions of grandeur, comes to mind. With more than 200 diagnoses listed in the bible of psychiatry, the *Diagnostic and Statistical Manual of Mental Disorders*, published by the American Psychiatric Association, there are lots of options.

The more precise numbers commonly used in modern medicine, such as the amounts of any one of hundreds of substances measured in blood, urine, or other body fluids or tissues, are generally reported with a range of normal values, but how the laboratories determine what that normal range should be and how they report them may influence your care dramatically. The normal or reference ranges are generally determined by encompassing the values found in 95 percent of apparently healthy volunteers and are therefore very dependent on who volunteers to be in the control population; if a patient has fifty tests done as a batch (many automated chemical analyses are set up to measure a number of blood components simultaneously), there is a high probability that at least one value will be reported as abnormal. That may well lead to a lot of further investigation to determine why you are abnormal, when in fact you are completely normal. Ninety-year-old men are seldom included in the volunteers used to determine the laboratory reference ranges of serum testosterone, so we really do not know what the normal range is in this population.

Many laboratory tests are now reported in an improved format and are adjusted for age, gender, and specific situations such as pregnancy or menopause, and are reported alongside the "desirable" or "healthy" normal range, but even this creates interpretation problems. If you are diabetic, for example, the desirable or healthy range of serum cholesterol is lower than if you are not. A late-blooming teenager with a growth spurt at age nineteen will show a high level of serum alkaline phosphatase, an enzyme measured to assess you for bone or liver disease, even with the age-adjusted reference range.

In other areas, the whole concept of normal becomes clouded by a laudable desire to keep you healthy and free of disease. For example, most of us start to lose some mineral from our bones in our thirties, which can lead in later years to osteoporosis. This loss is accelerated with certain diseases and drug treatments and in women after menopause. There is now a huge industry to measure bone mineral density and to treat this mineral loss to prevent fractures in the frail elderly. Bone mineral density is typically reported with the results compared to the expected gender-specific peak value (T-score) and also with reference to the expected value for your age and gender (Z-score). However, there is a natural tendency for physicians wanting to reduce your future fracture risk to look only at how far your bone mineral density is below the peak value for your gender, and that T-score is likely to become more negative as you age. Ignoring the definitional problem of what is normal, there are thousands of "normal" people being treated to prevent fractures who may not benefit. If a patient's life expectancy because of other diseases is two years, why should she be taking a drug designed to prevent her from developing osteoporosis and possible fracture in ten years? Furthermore, there is now some evidence that the treatment itself, if continued for several years, while increasing the desired number in a bone mineral density test, may actually increase your risk of certain specific fractures.[4] However, treating the number on your bone mineral density is much easier than treating you, and the same can be said about treating almost any of the myriad of numbers that physicians have reported to them daily.

A second problem with treating numbers rather than the patient is that of looking at the numbers in isolation, with not enough regard for physical symptoms. Several examples follow.

One complication of severe liver disease is hepatic encephalopathy, a usually reversible state of altered consciousness ranging from mild confusion to deep coma. Its cause is very complex. Long treatises and books have been written about what chemical alterations are responsible, but there is no doubt that ammonia, although not the only culprit, is involved in some way. The menu of lab testing in most hospitals includes a check box that makes it all too easy to request the measurement of blood ammonia levels.

As an experienced old workhorse hepatology consultant, I often received phone calls from peripheral centres to discuss the care of patients with complex liver disease. The conversations frequently included concerns that the blood ammonia level was rising. However, if the patient is mentally normal, the blood ammonia level is usually irrelevant. Unless the specimen is kept on ice, most of the ammonia measured in the lab is generated in the test tube of blood on the way to the lab, as ammonia is generated from other blood components at room temperature. In any case, there is virtually no correlation between the blood ammonia level and the patient's mental functioning–the brain concentrations are important, but the blood levels are not. If the blood ammonia level is normal but the patient is comatose, she needs treatment for hepatic encephalopathy; if the ammonia level is high but the patient is alert and oriented, she does not need the treatment. Whenever I pointed this out, and suggested that they stop measuring the ammonia, there was usually a long and disappointed pause at the other end of the line. Suddenly, there was nothing to treat; or rather, there was no number to treat, but there was a real patient to treat and monitor. But it is far easier to sit at the computer screen and graph the trend in the serum ammonia level than to do a mental status examination of the patient to determine if there may be some subtle changes in his mental functioning.

Treating numbers in isolation becomes more of a temptation as new, more accurate tests become available. A colleague of mine is currently involved in a study to accurately measure kidney function in liver transplant patients. This involves injection of a radioactive tracer to precisely determine the patient's glomerular filtration rate, a recognized standard test of kidney function. It is a more precise and accurate reflection of the patient's kidney function than the standard and more convenient blood measurement of serum creatinine, but is also more time-consuming, requires exposure to a small amount of radiation, and gives the accurate number at only one specific time. In contrast, the serum creatinine can be measured daily if needed, with one small tube of blood. The real kidney function may vary widely over time. The goal of the newer test is to allow the physician to more accurately alter the drug regimen of the patient to minimize the risk of progressive kidney failure. However, there is a danger that the number will be considered in isolation, without considering a host of factors that should also be considered when juggling the regimen of drug therapy that these patients need, including such factors as other side effects of the medication, and other diseases that may coexist, including diabetes, high blood pressure, and obesity. The goal is laudable, but there is a danger that treating the accurate number will result in not treating the patient appropriately.

Monitoring blood drug levels is a standard and useful practice in numerous situations, not the least of which is to ensure that patients are actually taking medication as prescribed. Even this can be a problem—one resourceful young woman who had been experiencing bouts of rejection of her liver transplant in spite of good blood levels of the drug finally confided that she only took the drug the night before her blood tests, as she knew that it would be tested! Other uses include the monitoring of seizure disorders, many drug therapies for various heart diseases, and monitoring the therapy after organ transplantation to ensure that the patient is not at undue risk of developing organ rejection. Here again, however, looking at the numbers without considering other factors that could account for symptoms can lead to inappropriate or even dangerous treatment. One common problem is that the levels must be timed in relation to the last dose to be interpreted at all, and getting the blood sample taken at the critical time is difficult. If the time interval is incorrect, the change in dosage to raise or lower the blood level may be quite dangerous. When I was on call for the hepatology service, I often got phone calls to report the levels of anti-rejection drugs in transplant patients from all over Canada, with a request for orders to adjust the dosing accordingly. In many cases, I had not seen the patient for months or years, had no idea what side effects of the medication the patient was experiencing, and had no idea what other problems he had. While the main purpose of the drug monitoring in these patients is to prevent rejection or toxicity, a host of other factors is equally important in determining whether or not the patient is at risk for rejection or other medication-related problems. I often refused to order a change in the dosage until I found out more about the individual patient's unique circumstances.

Drug manufacturers have yet another reason for recommending monitoring drug levels in blood: they can thereby sell more of the drug. If a patient's drug level is found to be below what is considered desirable, i.e., "sub-therapeutic," the medical practitioner's response is likely to be to order an increase in the dosage. But a blood level is often sub-therapeutic simply because the blood sample was taken too long after the last dose, or may even be an indication to reduce the usage. For example, if a patient with a seizure disorder has not had a seizure in years and has a blood level of Dilantin below what is considered therapeutic, the correct response may be to try to reduce or discontinue its use, since the patient is doing well, and may not need it at all, rather than to increase the dose. Similarly, the cardiac patient on digoxin for atrial fibrillation who has a resting pulse rate of 60 does not need the digoxin dosage changed, regardless of the fact that the blood level may be considered too low. And a patient who has normal liver function and no symptoms years after liver transplantation does not need an increase in the dosage of the anti-rejection drugs cyclosporine or tacrolimus even if the blood levels are reported to be below the target level, or even in the undetectable range.

The above situations illustrate the potential for problems in treating numbers and ignoring the patient. This is not to say that numbers are not useful, although in some situations, a number is not needed for diagnosis. In other situations, numbers are useful in determining or validating treatments. For example, diseases that produce obvious anatomical abnormalities, such as colon cancer or coronary artery blockage, do not need numbers to diagnose the disease, although numbers indicating the size of the cancer or the degree of narrowing of the artery will be useful to determine treatment.

For other diseases, the use of numbers is largely what gives modern medicine some scientific validity. Endless papers discuss how one number is better than another in treating a specific disease. If you are diabetic, for example, a hemoglobin A1C level (a reflection of long-term control of blood glucose levels) of 5 percent is likely to lead to a longer, healthier life than one of 8 percent. The MELD (Model of Endstage Liver Disease) score, mathematically derived from the results of three common blood tests, accurately reflects the likelihood of dying of chronic liver disease in the next three months, and has been mandated by the Institute of Medicine in the United States as one of the critical factors in determining who qualifies to receive a donated liver. The blood level of PSA is a reasonable predictor of the probability of having prostate cancer (see Chapter 3), although poor at predicting its aggressiveness. A score on a Beck Depression Inventory, a twenty-one-item, self-reported questionnaire, can be scientifically used by a psychiatrist to determine whether or not a prescribed antidepressant is effective. There are literally thousands of examples like this in modern practice where the number, whether from a blood test or from a scientifically validated scoring system, is crucial in your doctor's deciding what should be done.

In some cases, there is no number to treat, only symptoms, and a scientifically trained physician may react in one of three ways. The first is to dismiss the symptoms as of no significance. A well-known Herman® cartoon shows the doctor across the desk from the patient with the caption, "Your tests are all normal. Get lost." The second is to simply treat the symptoms, often without any numeric diagnosis, as when, for example, you show up with a nasty cough during flu season and are given a prescription for a simple cough suppressant. However, some subjective symptoms unassociated with any specific laboratory abnormality are worthy of scientific study, and without a number that is difficult. The third reaction of a scientist, then, is to create a number. Several examples follow.

Severe diffuse itching, to the point of literally scratching oneself raw, is a common and often neglected feature of certain kinds of chronic liver disease. Some people become psychotic because of sleep deprivation from scratching, and at least two people I knew committed suicide when seemingly nothing could be done to relieve their itching. When I tried to study the problem, no number was correlated with the severity of the itching, so we created one. Borrowing from social sciences and other studies of subjective symptoms, we used a visual analogue scale—a line on which the subjects each day marked the severity of their itch on a scale of 0 to 100. Using this artificial number along with other trial design features, we were able to show scientifically that an old drug, rifampin, is very effective for a new use, relieving itch in these people.[5] Hardly a cure for cancer, but it is one of the accomplishments I am most proud of. However, visual analogue scales, although extensively used in research, are not used routinely in most clinical day-to-day care situations. There is, therefore, no number associated with itching.

Furthermore, liver patients often do not make the connection of the itching to their liver disease, and the physicians trained and oriented to treat numbers often fail to ask about itching. As a result, many people suffer for years with this miserable symptom without realizing that there is effective treatment. As an aside, fierce debates ensued—after this study stimulated interest in researching itch—about the best ways of putting a number on the severity of itching. Some researchers argued that their fancy scratching frequency monitors adapted to be worn on fingers, are a better measure than a visual analogue scale. To me, scratching is, at least conceptually, a response to itching that higher brain centres can modify and is therefore not as clean a measurement of itchiness as the visual analogue scale. However, the real point is that we needed something numerical to scientifically study a symptom as subjective as itching.

Another example of deliberately developing numbers to study a function comes from an unusual subject area. Excessive flatulence or excessively aromatic flatulence is a very common complaint that family physicians and gastroenterologists alike deal with. This complaint could not really be investigated scientifically until some number was attached to what is normal in this form of natural gas production. Dr. Michael Levitt did just that. In an unusual career studying everything about intestinal gas, from frequency of passage to volume to composition, in volunteers, he produced numbers that can be attached to this normal function. The surprising results are that while men outperform women in frequency, women tend to produce the most offensive emissions. One would not suspect this from most casual conversations. Furthermore, most patients with irritable bowel syndrome who complain of excessive gas actually do not produce more or more frequently than the normal volunteers, but have a heightened awareness of the progress of the gas to the outside world, a kind of increased sensitivity setting on their brain's anal monitor.

With Dr. Levitt's work, there are now numbers to indicate what is normal. As an aside, it seems fitting for such an eclectic researcher to produce a son, Steven, one of the authors of *Freakenomics* and *Superfreakenomics*, with equally eccentric research interests (is eccentric brilliance hereditary?). In spite of Dr. Levitt's gas-breaking work, however, keeping track of how often one emits, or worse, collecting one's emissions for analysis, has not really caught on in mainstream medicine for some reason. As a result, there is still a widespread tendency for doctors to dismiss such complaints as having no association with real disease—there are no numbers that are easily obtained or measured in a laboratory to treat, and not surprisingly, these patients are among the least satisfied with the care they get from their doctors.

In some cases, the lack of a number leads to the temptation by scientifically trained physicians to dismiss a condition of some importance as not being a disease at all. In the Diagnostic and Statistical Manual of mental disorders (DSM–IV™), for example, there is no mention of numbers in the criteria to diagnose the post-traumatic stress disorder. Does this mean that it is really not a disease? The absence of numbers certainly makes it, and the treatment of it, hard to study scientifically, and hard-core scientists are prone to conclude that it should not be included in the ever-expanding list of new "diseases"; after all, this is a psychological "disease" and not a medical one, is it not? However, the sufferers have real symptoms and are certainly deserving of society's help. Meanwhile, although sex addiction is not currently in the DSM–IV list of disorders, a working party is allegedly discussing its inclusion in the next edition due to be published in 2012. Proponents of its inclusion point out that the chemical changes in the brain with orgasm mimic those of a heroin high, so there seems to be a scientific basis for including it as a true addiction. Opponents point out that the behaviour is simply an exaggeration of a normal impulse. There are no readily available numbers to attach to this "disease," but if it is ever officially recognized as such, you can be sure there will be some scoring system (pardon the pun) developed to allow it to be studied scientifically.

With the limited budgets of publicly funded health-care systems, the inclusion of more and more "diseases" in the list of conditions that are covered becomes problematic. I have no answers for this phenomenon of "medicalization" of what are often social or psychological problems. However, it does not seem wise to limit the list of diseases that are recognized as such to those that have numbers associated with them, although that certainly makes it easier to study them. Perhaps one solution would be to remove one condition every time a new disease is listed or defined. We could start with some of those other nebulous DSM-IV disorders that are official diseases, such as "female orgasmic disorder" or "hypoactive sexual desire disorder." If the criteria for calling something a disease is that an M.D. is best qualified to treat it, I doubt that either of these—or many other conditions without any numerical abnormality—would qualify.

Treating patients is a complicated business that involves far more than treating the numbers generated from a laboratory test, an imaging study, or a scoring system derived from some combination of tests. Experienced wise physicians treat real people while not ignoring the numbers that come from their test results. But doctors who prefer to treat numbers rather than people may find that many of their patients die with all of their numbers within the normal range.

Notes

1. Frederick C.W. Wu, et al., "Identification of Late-Onset Hypogonadism in Middle-Aged and Elderly Men," *New England Journal of Medicine* 363 (2010): 123–35.
2. Shehzad Basaria, et al., "Adverse Events Associated with Testosterone Administration," *New England Journal of Medicine* 363 (2010): 109–22.
3. William J. Bremner, "Testosterone Deficiency and Replacement in Older Men," *New England Journal of Medicine* 363 (2010): 189–91.
4. Brett A. Lenart, Dean G. Lorich, and Joseph M. Lane, "Atypical Fractures of the Femoral Diaphysis in Postmenopausal Women Taking Alendronate," *New England Journal of Medicine* 358 (2008): 1304–06.
5. Cameron N. Ghent and S.G. Carruthers, "Treatment of Pruritus of Cholestasis in Primary Biliary Cirrhosis with Rifampin," *Gastroenterology* 94 (1988): 488–93.

℞ 13

Diagnosis

Medical mystery problem-solving

Dr. Gregory House, Hugh Laurie in real life, the irascible star of Fox TV's award-winning show *House*, can come up with a diagnosis to explain any set of symptoms with amazing accuracy and often with seemingly only the flimsiest clues. It seems to help that his colleagues often give the patient the wrong treatment and that the disastrous results of those treatments give him the critical clue that he needs to make the surprise diagnosis. It also seems to help if the patient lies about the history, and if the disease the patient actually has is a rare one that mimics a common one. He can seemingly juggle a few dozen different variables in his inquisitive mind and has unlimited knowledge of the medical literature. He does not mind being wrong on the first guess but always comes up with the correct diagnosis before his colleagues' inappropriate treatment kills the patient. It is clear that he is a narcotic addict and that his diagnostic acumen is apparently increased when his brain is well saturated with oxycodone. He is a self-professed diagnostician (although there is no such recognized medical specialty).

No mere mortal doctor is likely to match the skills of Dr. House, but most doctors spend a considerable amount of their time trying to match symptoms to a diagnosis. Their training should include not only how to make accurate diagnoses but to recognize when it may be inappropriate to continue searching and when to recruit help from a colleague for a diagnosis.

What is a diagnosis? In basic terms, it is the resolution of a problem presented by findings or symptoms. In actual fact, however, there can be many levels to that resolution. It can be as simple as finding that a patient with a cough has dullness on percussion of the chest over one area of a lung along with crackles heard with a stethoscope in the same area, indicating a pneumonia that can be easily confirmed with a chest x-ray. The symptoms, signs, and imaging findings are all explained with one word, although the level of resolution of the problem can sometimes be extended if a particular causative organism can be identified. This usually requires some further testing, but at times, the history (if obtained) will provide the answer. A child with a pneumonia who has just broken out in the characteristic rash of chickenpox almost certainly has pneumonia caused by the chickenpox virus. This requires little diagnostic acumen if the child, and not just the x-ray, is actually examined.

More complex diagnoses require more levels of resolution and are frequently made in the absence of any outward symptoms. If routine checkup blood tests indicate low hemoglobin and MCV (a measure of the size of your red blood cells) levels, you will be diagnosed with anemia—one level of diagnostic resolution. In the absence of more levels of resolution, this will not help you much. You may have no symptoms of the colon cancer that is causing you to lose blood slowly. Unless your physician orders further tests to determine the cause, the diagnosis of anemia is incomplete; failure to investigate the cause may well lead to the growth of the cancer until it finally produces bowel symptoms, at which point it is often incurable. The next level of diagnostic resolution of that anemia—once a surgeon removes part of your colon, and a pathologist examines the specimen—may well be a cancer involving the colon at the splenic flexure (where it turns downward near the spleen) with or without spread to lymph nodes. When that pathology examination shows that the cancer is arising in a benign colon polyp, a new level of diagnostic resolution has been reached. Although pathologists like to think they have the last word in diagnostic resolution, an even higher resolution of the diagnosis may be possible, if genetic testing is done, and you are found to have an acquired mutation of a gene that causes you to develop colonic polyps and colon cancer. And even that level may be refined further if an epidemiologist shows that you have developed that gene mutation because of exposure to environmental toxins unique to your workplace.

The processes above describe the levels of resolution that must be kept in mind in any discussion of the concept of a diagnosis. In the above scenario, the final diagnosis may then be: iron deficiency anemia secondary to gastrointestinal blood loss, secondary to a poorly differentiated T2 N0 adenocarcinoma of the splenic flexure, secondary to an acquired genetic mutation, secondary to environmental toxin exposure. Not even Dr. House is likely to be able to take the diagnostic resolution process that far!

Sometimes a diagnosis may not seem to resolve the problem or symptom, but simply restates the symptom. In many such situations, a further level of resolution is of no benefit and may, in fact, be detrimental to the patient. A diagnosis of low back pain NYD (not yet diagnosed) is simply restating what the patient is complaining about. While this seems unfulfilling to the patient, trying to be more precise and taking the diagnosis to the next level of resolution may not be possible or wise. A plethora of "abnormalities" is likely to be reported if the patient with chronic low back pain is subjected to imaging studies such as magnetic resonance imaging (MRI) examinations, but the relationship of the findings to the pain is difficult to establish. In fact, the information gained by trying to be more precise with this symptom is so problematic that the American College of Physicians and The American Pain Society have recommended that an MRI not be done on a routine basis in the investigation of chronic low back pain,[1] as it frequently leads to unnecessary and unhelpful further investigations and unneeded surgery. This is not to suggest that there is no appropriate treatment for low back pain NYD; if you accept that you are a member of a species that is still adjusting to the relatively recent adoption of a bipedal posture and locomotion, the back pain can be appropriately treated without a precise anatomical diagnosis. At times, making a diagnosis at a higher level of resolution does not do the patient a favour.

Training medical students to make accurate diagnoses is obviously a crucial part of their education. Traditionally, students are taught that the starting point for making a diagnosis, at any level of resolution, is a careful, complete history and physical examination. The process is to collect all of the relevant information from the patient or other source, record all the normal or abnormal findings on a careful and complete examination, and then integrate the information and findings with their knowledge about disease processes to come up with a logical explanation of the symptoms or findings: a diagnosis.

But how careful and how complete should this information-gathering and examination process be? There are literally hundreds of questions for the patient that have some validity in coming to the right diagnosis or diagnoses, depending on the symptoms and circumstances, and the list of possible tests on physical examination is equally long. Obviously some tailoring of the questions and some focusing of the examination to the complaints of the patient is necessary, and our students learn this time-saving strategy quickly once they set up practice, if not before. When starting out in this business, however, it may be necessary to teach students how to cast a wide net. One of the difficulties I always had in teaching history-taking to students was that we taught them to ask a long list of questions before they had any basic knowledge about how to interpret the answers. Some focus is needed to avoid spending all day doing one history and physical examination. No one I know routinely tests all twelve cranial nerves for every new patient they see, although I was taught how to do so and taught others how to do so.

Dr. Lawrence Weed formalized the traditional approach above and modified it, developing the Problem-Oriented Medical Record in 1969. In this approach, a long list of problems to be resolved is recorded rather than specific diagnoses at any level of resolution. Most trainees today still loosely follow the POMR format when recording a history, with the word "problem" appearing so often that it becomes a problem. The logic behind the teaching of the collect-the-complete-database approach to the beginners is to give them enough experience to learn what they can and should safely ignore. But it takes some judgment and experience to differentiate between relevant and irrelevant features of the patient's past history. Be patient with the medical student asking all those seemingly stupid questions—she or he may not yet have the experience to sort out what is relevant.

One difficulty with this shotgun method of collecting an enormous amount of information and then trying to sort it out later is that few patients will end up with only one diagnosis. Using this system, several problems can be identified in almost any adult—usually at least one per decade of adult life. However, collecting all of the information and organizing it into problems or diagnoses later may well lead to a twenty-item problem list that is replete with past inactive problems that do not deserve any consideration at the time of presentation of a new set of symptoms. Most people, if subjected to enough questions and tests, will have *some* abnormality or at least a past problem identified, even if it is not relevant to the current situation or complaint. It is, however, an axiom of medicine to never make two diagnoses if you can possibly explain all the symptoms with one. If one can intellectually link the current complaint with something in the patient's past history, it is best to know about those past problems. For example, a past history of adequately treated tuberculosis is very relevant if a patient on medication that suppresses the immune system develops a cough and fever, but it is totally irrelevant if he is being treated for a broken arm. That long list of problems or diagnoses may be important in some circumstances but may also serve to just divert the doctor's attention away from the patient's current complaint.

A second difficulty with this approach of collecting all the information first and then trying to formulate a diagnosis is that it is all wrong, or is at least the reverse of the actual process used by all experienced clinicians—except, of course, for Dr. House. In most situations, the diagnosis, at least at some level of resolution, is obvious, or is made by the patient, or even, such as with a diagnosis of obesity, by the weigh scale that automatically calculates the body mass index as the patient is being checked in. Many diagnoses, again at some level of resolution, are obvious from simple procedures such as taking a blood pressure reading, asking a few standard interview questions, or doing minimal standard blood or urine tests. In specialty practice, prior investigations have already reached some level of diagnostic resolution before the patient is seen. This may be as vague as weight loss NYD, or as specific as genetic hemochromatosis due to homozygosity for the C282y mutation of the HFE gene—in lay terms, excess absorption of iron due to a specific gene mutation inherited from both parents.

Even in the mystery cases that are common only on *House*, the process of collecting all of the information and then analyzing it in exquisite detail to come up with a brilliant, unifying diagnosis is the reverse of the process used by experienced clinicians. Even if they were taught the traditional approach of collecting all of the information and then scratching their heads to put it all together, they typically mentally formulate some hypothesis about what is wrong with the patient in the first few seconds of a first encounter, or even before that, if they spend some time reviewing the information that is already available from the chart, x-rays, or nursing notes. There are two approaches even to this initial mental process. I watched many trainees using the first approach of spending an inordinate amount of time poring over notes, lab reports, and imaging studies before seeing the patient, establishing a hypothesis before eyeballing the patient. I preferred to see the patient first, using the information provided by others to fill in the blanks in the data, reviewing that information in front of the patient, checking the accuracy of those reports with her. This approach achieves two valuable goals. First, the information may not be accurate or up to date and may need to be corrected. Second, spending the time with the patient let her know that I was actually working on her problem and made her appreciate the amount of time spent on her case.

After forming their initial hypothesis, most physicians follow this second approach. They test their instincts by interviewing the patient and examining him, stopping the process when they have collected enough information to either confirm or refute their initial hunch. If information comes to light that completely refutes the initial hypothesis, a new hypothesis is formed and tested in the same way; this process may be repeated several times until the tentative diagnosis is deemed to sufficiently explain all the symptoms. What then follows is the collection of additional information that may be relevant to confirm the hypothesis, determine how severe the disease is, and determine what other diseases may be impacting the symptoms, or what factors may influence the further plans for treatment—a limited and focused form of the broad inquiry and examination that we taught those beginners, but occurring after the initial diagnosis rather than before.

The really challenging unusual cases where each hypothesis the clinician forms is proven wrong by some bit of information that comes to light during the history and physical examination, or subsequent laboratory testing or imaging, are what make Dr. House look brilliant. They are also the ones that challenge the skills of real-life clinicians and lead to fun games of diagnostic one-upmanship. All clinicians love to be known as the detective who cracked the case that mystified his colleagues. However, it is not the clinician who, like Dr. House, can keep track of more variables than his colleagues that usually solves such true mysteries. Rather than ordering more tests, the solution to the mystery often depends on a review of the information already available, minus the biases and the narrowing of perspectives that lead to the initial incorrect hypotheses. In these rare true mysteries, the most likely means of making the brilliant diagnosis is to start from the beginning—redo the history and physical examination, without overloading one's brain with the sometimes erroneous information already on file. It may be necessary to use the unbiased brain of a colleague, particularly if social distance factors (see Chapter 7) have limited the initial doctor's ability to consider all of the possibilities objectively. The crucial clue may well be obvious and already in the record, but overlooked because of information overload.

In the Internet age, patients can become remarkably efficient at diagnosing even rare diseases. For example, the mother of a preteen girl diagnosed an extremely rare condition called hepatic protoporphyria in her daughter and had the testing done to confirm it after many doctors had failed to figure out why the girl developed severe burns to her mouth from exposure to dental lamps and second-degree skin burns from minimal exposure to the sun. The only part of the diagnostic process left to me when I saw the child was to figure out which gene responsible for this disorder she had obtained from her mother and which from her father. Genetic testing for this kind of diagnosis can at times be a delicate business, but fortunately the testing did confirm that her mother's husband was the child's father. Although many physicians become very indignant when the patient proffers a self-diagnosis, these Internet searchers deserve to be taken seriously, if only to spend some extra time to discuss why their own diagnosis for their symptoms is erroneous.

Another negative of the process of collecting abundant information about your illness and symptoms is that it becomes almost impossible to integrate it all into a unifying diagnosis because of information overload. Malcolm Gladwell has argued that the information overload that comes from doing too much investigation and too much thinking may actually impair the process of coming to the correct conclusion.[2] The collect-all-the-data approach often results in so much information overload that there is then no attempt to put any hypothesis in play at all, and the default way out is to go through a process of ruling out any number of possibilities. This may involve slapping an investigative protocol (see Chapter 11) onto the chart after the information has been collected without any consideration as to whether or not any of the possible diagnoses that may be discovered with that protocol are relevant to the patient's symptoms. This not only increases the information overload, but also presents the danger that you may be found to have something that you did not really need to know about or want to know about. It seems far better to make a hypothesis and then prove that it is wrong and move on to the next possibility than it is to go through this process of elimination.

"Rule out" are probably the two most significant words in medical lingo to account for wasteful expenditure of money to get more (often irrelevant) information and delays in arriving at the diagnosis and treatment, and the resulting further expenditure on treating problems that are found but that may not need any treatment. It is appropriate to rule out any number of coexisting conditions if you already have a diagnosis and it is necessary to exclude other diseases whose presence may be equally important to your future health or may impact the treatment of the main problem. However, before using the rule-out option, a critical question needs to be asked: "Will the finding of the condition being tested for explain any of the symptoms or impact the treatment of them?" Often the rule-out process is used before there has been any rule-in process with the excuse that it is expected in specialty practice to exclude all serious diseases within that specialty—hence the urologist cannot resist the temptation to order a PSA test, even if prostate cancer would not explain any of the presenting symptoms.

The prevalent process of "rule out" can lead to serious negative consequences, such as being found to have an untreatable genetic disease that causes you anxiety for the rest of your life, or finding something that leads to a denial of a later application for life insurance. Often the rule-out option is used rather than a rule-in approach with an eye to covering the possibility of missing something that a legal wizard might question your doctor about. This is neither problem-solving nor good exercise for the brain. This "rule-in/rule-out" process is now not limited to testing by physicians—with the human genome mapping, you may soon (for a hefty fee) be able to submit a saliva sample to a genetic testing company and get a confidential on-line printout of your propensity to develop any number of diseases. Do you really want to find out the exact probability of your developing Alzheimer's disease in the next ten years? Is there not something positive and very human about learning to live with uncertainty?

It is not my intention to argue against expecting your doctor to do a thorough history and physical examination. Most errors in levels of diagnosis and treatment occur not because of neglecting to order some imaging study or blood test, but because of failure to do enough inquiry and examination to form a complete picture of what may be going on in addition to the major diagnosis.

An example from my area of practice may clarify this multistep process. The hypothesis that the patient has hepatitis C may be adequately tested in a few minutes with a review of blood test results, an analysis of the symptoms and risk factors, and a brief examination for outward signs of chronic liver disease. The main diagnosis is then already made, but the evaluation has only begun. Further questioning may reveal that the patient also has arthritis or a chronic skin rash, suggesting an interesting complication of hepatitis C. Or examination may reveal blisters on the backs of the hands, suggesting a different complication of this infection. Discussion of past medical problems may uncover a history of severe depression, coronary artery disease, or a history of excessive bleeding with minor procedures, all relevant factors in a comprehensive assessment of hepatitis C. All of these items are vital to an adequate assessment and treatment of the patient—but not to the first-order diagnosis of hepatitis C.

There are some situations for which no diagnosis is possible, and where trying to form one may even be detrimental to the patient. Except on *House*, a situation where there are no clues to a diagnosis at any level of resolution for someone with an obviously life-threatening illness is really quite rare. Understandably, this creates consternation for the patient, the family, and the attending health-care workers. There is an urgency to make some sense of the symptoms as they worsen, and a tendency to scramble for a unifying diagnosis even if and when it seems unlikely that there will be any hope of treatment that will prevent the patient's impending death. This is particularly a problem when an aggressive widespread malignancy is suspected but not proven. Many such patients spend their last days being shuffled back and forth from one hospital department to another for imaging studies, diagnostic procedures, and biopsies of different organs in a desperate attempt to prove that they have some terminal untreatable illness before they die. Whether they die with or without that diagnosis may be more important for the family than for the patient. But the diagnosis can usually be established after death by a thorough autopsy, although it is a myth that the autopsy always provides a final answer. That may be true on *CSI*, but not in the real world. Often an autopsy reveals a dozen different diagnoses, but does not reveal which disease process killed the patient. And many nonagenarians die suddenly without any apparent diagnosis and with no explanation found even at autopsy. Not a bad way to go, if you are ninety-five—unless you are already ninety-four, and healthy enough to want another ten years.

Notes

1. R. Chou, A. Qaseem, and V. Snow, et al., "Diagnosis and Treatment of Low Back Pain: A Joint Clinical Practice Guideline from the American College of Physicians and the American Pain Society," *Annals of Internal Medicine* 147 (2007): 478–91.
2. M. Gladwell, *Blink* (Boston: Little, Brown and Company, 2005).

Rx 14

Tax Dollars at Work

Rational and irrational rationing

An attractive blonde woman in her mid-twenties[1] came to my office with an unusual request. I had known her since she was a scrawny, yellow, ten-year-old child; she had never known what it was like to be healthy until her chronic liver disease was cured with a liver transplant in her late teens. As a result of the disease, she had not developed normally, and had almost no breasts. She wanted me to draft a letter to indicate that her "mammary hypoplasia" was due to her chronic liver disease, that this was adversely affecting her health, and that it was medically necessary to have this corrected with augmentation surgery (implants). If I could convince the bureaucrats at the public funding agency for health care in Ontario, the Ontario Health Insurance Plan (OHIP), of the veracity of all three points, they would then consider her implants a medical necessity. The Ontario taxpayer would then pay for the service, waiving the general rule that this is an elective cosmetic procedure paid for by the patient. The cause-and-effect relationship between her chronic liver disease and her flat chest was quite certain; her liver disease had prevented the hormonal changes that result in breast development, but this could not be scientifically verified now that the problem had been corrected. She insisted that her lack of breasts was a constant reminder of her chronic invalidism in her growing years and that she needed implants to feel and function normally as an adult. The young man who accompanied her made it clear that the prairie-like contour of her chest was not important to him—he loved her anyway and planned to marry her. Your call—should I write the letter? To do so would mean making an exception to the usual economic rationing of this service. Vote now!

Rationing is a part of all health care everywhere. Although politics, geography, science, and social norms or social distances (see Chapter 7) are factors, decisions are largely based on economic considerations and responsible expenditure of taxpayer money, at least in publicly funded systems. The basic question being asked is: What are the boundaries of "medically necessary" services that justify expenditures of the taxpayer's money? Economic factors dominate discussion in the debates, whether they are argued by the newly minted specialists in health-care economics, by politicians, who tend to deny the existence of rationing, or by front-line workers who debate and research the costs of one treatment versus another for hundreds of diseases. Is it cost-effective and better to use the newer, slightly more effective antidepressants than the older ones that are cheaper but may take longer to reach the desired goal? What combination of medications is best for initial treatment of newly diagnosed AIDS? Which of these should be listed in hospital and public formularies? These economic questions about rationing of health-care services pervade the discussion at every level from the individual doctor-patient encounter to international meetings. And is it better to provide this under-endowed young woman with the implants she says she needs to forget her tragic teens than to provide psychological counselling for her?

Health-care rationing and politics is a volatile combination. Elected officials are reluctant to acknowledge that they ever deny the population that elected them any medical services, and, especially in Canada, the myth of accessible, free, universal, publicly funded health care is a sacred cow that all politicians pay lip service to. But failing to provide funds to keep a rural emergency room open, delaying the approval of the best agents for the provincial formulary for treatment of hepatitis B in those on welfare, or delisting neonatal circumcision as an insured service under the provincial health insurance plan are all forms of rationing of health-care services. In situations such as closing the rural emergency room, it is absolute rationing; you can't get the service if it isn't there. In other cases, you can get the service if you are willing and able to pay for it, as in the case of the breast implants, the newest antiviral medication for hepatitis B, and the neonatal circumcision. The last was delisted from OHIP in 1994 and costs about $150, and the delisting had almost no impact on the frequency of its performance.

In other cases, the prohibition extends even to those who are willing and able to pay, but unable to purchase the service because the authorities have prohibited it. If you suffer from multiple sclerosis and are convinced that you need the angioplasty-like surgery devised by Dr. Zamboni for what he calls chronic cerebrospinal venous insufficiency, you will probably have to travel to Lebanon or India and pay for the surgery out of your own pocket. Most hospitals in North America prohibit their staff surgeons from doing experimental surgery outside of clinical trials, and even Dr. Zamboni, the media darling who described the treatment first and has gone on a world tour to promote it, is still only recommending further clinical trials. However, had he followed the advice of Dr. Tom Chalmers to randomize the first patient within a trial when a new potential therapy is introduced,[2] we would now have the answer about whether or not this therapy is effective. This example illustrates well the interaction of politics, geography, science, and economics that often are involved in rationing. The politics includes reactions to pressure groups lobbying to include the treatment as an insured service. The geography includes the fact that no one in North America has much experience with the surgical techniques—if the proposed trial of this treatment funded in part by the MS Society of Canada shows it is of no benefit and therefore should not be an insured service, Dr. Zamboni can always claim that they simply did not do the surgery the right way. The science includes skepticism about the possibility that a relatively unknown Italian surgeon may have made a major discovery related to a disease totally outside of his field of expertise. There will be considerable professional jealousy from the neurologists who have devoted their lives to studying this disease if Dr. Zamboni's treatment is shown to be effective. There are also the ever-present debates about how solid the scientific evidence of benefit needs to be before something becomes a non-rationed standard treatment. As for the economic aspects, Dr. Zamboni is not offering the surgery free of charge, although he probably did not invoice his wife, who was one of his first patients to undergo his procedure. As of this writing, you can book your treatment on-line for about $6,000 U.S., not counting travel costs, to have your MS cured in India or Lebanon.[3]

The reach of politics can have international implications, as shown by the raging debates over foreign aid when the aid money may include support for abortion services in Third World countries. I am not stating any personal position on the morality of abortions, but the Canadian government's refusal to supply foreign aid to programs that include abortion services is a form of de facto rationing of health services to poor women in other countries based on Canadian domestic politics and on the moral positions of politicians and their supporters at home. It seems ironic that Canada has honoured Dr. Henry Morgentaler, its most famous abortion proponent, with membership in the Order of Canada and allows quite liberal access to abortions for Canadian women on Canadian soil, but seems to regard similar access in foreign countries as unconscionable. The contrast with the actions of the United States could not be sharper. The domestic access to abortion is much more restrictive there than in Canada, and abortion services are rationed or drastically restricted by law in many parts of the country. However, their foreign aid explicitly funds programs providing abortion services in third world countries. The irony of Hillary Clinton, from a country with relatively restrictive rationing of abortion services compared to Canada, castigating Stephen Harper about Canada's foreign aid policy because it does not support abortion services in the Third World should be obvious to everyone. Pandering to the religious and political views of the minority of people who are actually responsible for the power of elected officials accounts for some of this contradictory decision-making. Currently, the groups in power are generally conservative and anti-abortion in Canada and liberal and pro-choice in the U.S. relative to the populations as a whole. The mistake we tend to make in this debate is to expect politicians to be consistent—to think that foreign policy should be consistent with domestic policy. But these inconsistencies have major global effects that result in massive and irrational rationing of health-care funding.

Health-care economics is a huge industry that developed in part because there are no easy answers to the problem of consistent rationing of services. Whether or not to cover some questionable treatments and services such as breast augmentation is only a minor part of what the experts consider. The bigger issue for them is how to decide the relative value of different interventions. In their decision-making, health-care economists at times seem to be explicitly putting a dollar value on a life, with the cost per year of life saved with various treatments a common calculation when new treatments are compared with older ones. To refine this further, they adjust this cost for quality of life; a common calculation related to various interventions is the cost per quality adjusted life-years saved, the quality adjusted life years (QALY), or the more narrowly defined health-related quality of life, the HRQALY. Elaborate questionnaires are used to assign numbers to these for comparative purposes (see Chapter 12). Alternatively, a time trade-off calculation, which essentially asks how much of your remaining life would you be willing to sacrifice to free yourself from a certain symptom or disease, is used in some studies.

An example might make the above discussion clearer. If you have ulcerative colitis, a chronic disease of the colon, you may decide to have your colon removed rather than suffer with chronic diarrhea. Keeping your colon also increases your risk of developing cancer in it. However, having your colon removed also has costs and risks and will leave you with an ileostomy or some kind of surgical reconstruction that is likely to leave you with at least some diarrhea. In utility studies of these options, you would be asked to put a value on each possible outcome, from dying in the operating room to being completely healthy. Hypothetically, would you choose another twenty years of chronic diarrhea or trade this off for *x* number of years with a convenient ileostomy that saves you the trouble of always checking out where the nearest washroom is? Any number of variables in the outcome measures can be taken into account in models describing the utility of having the surgery, and costs can be calculated for the various options to arrive at a cost per HRQALY.

There are two major problems with such economic models. First, assumptions used in the model may not fit with the reality. If the assumption is that the surgical risk of dying is 0.5 percent, but for you it is actually 5 percent, the rest of the calculations will be all wrong for your situation. Second, people are not very good at predicting the quality of their lives with some future chronic condition, such as having an ileostomy, until they are actually living in that state. Most healthy people who are asked to rate their quality of life with some hypothetical future chronic disease give it a lower rating than do those who have actually developed the disease.[4] Michael J. Fox describes himself as a lucky man[5]—lucky to have developed apparent Parkinson's disease at a young age, insisting that the quality of his life improved with that development. Most people with ulcerative colitis who eventually opt for surgery, with lingering fears that this may impair the quality of their lives, wonder afterward why it took them so long to decide, because the quality of their lives improves dramatically. While QALY and time-tradeoff studies are valuable in helping healthcare economists compare treatments, they have their limitations in determining whether a particular form of treatment should be abandoned or delisted from insurance plans, or available only to a particular population.

Most of the covert or overt discussion of rationing of medical care is confined to professional journals or scientific meetings. The state of Oregon, however, has taken this issue public, in the hopes that the rationing that the publicly funded Oregon Health Plan openly acknowledges as a fact of life will reflect the values of the residents of that state. Since 1992, they have, with extensive public and expert input and with due consideration of comparative value research, listed about 700 (the list changes every year) conditions and treatments in order of priority for funding. The state legislature draws a line each year on the list where the available money will run out, and supposedly treatments below this line are not funded for residents requiring public money for their care. This experiment has been watched intently around the world, but has had less effect on limiting costs than expected, and it has been severely criticized for inconsistencies. Furthermore, making the rationing explicit and public seems to have made it more difficult to implement, with the line between insured and uninsured services becoming more blurred; many exceptions are being made because of public outcries about specific uninsured services. About the best that can be said for the Oregon experiment is that it gives the policymakers a clear picture of what the residents of the state view as important priorities for their health spending, at least for those who cannot afford private comprehensive insurance. It would be interesting to estimate how much the social distance (see Chapter 7) between the average Oregonian and those who cannot afford private insurance comes into play in setting up the famous list—is it seen as acceptable to deny certain costly services to "them" as long as "we" still have access to those services?

The covert rationing that goes on at the doctor-patient level does have considerable impact and could have more if doctors spent more time discussing the rationale for their decisions with the patient. When the insured, "worried well" patient requests a routine screening ultrasound, or a blood test to measure the PSA level, the relative cost-effectiveness of doing the test is very high; spending some time to explain that may be as effective in reducing the costs as any explicit rationing at the macroeconomic level. For example, it used to be common to take a teenager with typical symptoms, signs, and routine laboratory tests indicating appendicitis directly from the emergency room to the operating room for removal of the offending appendix. Now a stop in the x-ray department for a CT scan is the usual practice, but is it cost-effective to do so? If we are really interested in rational rationing, we should be studying the utility of this practice and hundreds of other routines that have not had their utility properly studied.

Back to the young woman who requested the free breast implants. Should I, in the interest of cost containment, stick to the general rule that this is a cosmetic procedure that does not warrant coverage with the public insurance in Ontario? In the 2010 Oregon listing,[6] breast augmentation is number 636 of 678 conditions or treatments and is well below the cutoff line in their list of priorities for public funding. Should I write that letter? Is it "medically necessary" for her health to have this done? Medical necessity is the rather flexible subjective guideline used by the Ontario provincial insurance plan to include a procedure in the benefits they will pay for. Would I be acting irresponsibly with the Ontario taxpayer's money to facilitate expenditure of it for this service? I discussed the ethics of this without divulging all of the specifics with several colleagues, both male and female, and did not reach consensus. I did not ask enough people to determine whether or not the decision of the women depended on their own endowments, and it would have been difficult to quantify that—one does not usually ask friends and colleagues about their bra cup size. But I was concerned that refusing to write the recommendation letter would strain a longstanding doctor-patient relationship. I did write the carefully worded letter. She did get her publicly funded implants inserted, and she did continue to function normally as an adult, including having a couple of healthy children. But there was one consequence that I had not foreseen—with her new man-magnets, she got a job in a strip club. I doubt that any of the men she entertained there ever realized that they were looking at their tax dollars at work. Did the Ontario taxpayers get their money's worth? It's time for you to vote again.

Notes

1. A few nonessential details have been altered to protect my patient's identity. She also reviewed this manuscript after we no longer had a doctor-patient relationship, and enthusiastically consented to my telling her story.
2. T.C. Chalmers, "Randomize the First Patient," *New England Journal of Medicine* 107 (1977): 296–97.
3. www.placidway.com advertisement, accessed August 20, 2010.
4. This phenomenon has been known since at least 1978, and is attributed in part to underestimating one's own adaptability to chronic disease. See D.L. Sackett and G.W. Torrance, "The Utility of Different Health States as Perceived by the General Public," *Journal of Chronic Diseases* 31 (1978): 697–704. Or for a drier but more complex explanation of this, see S. Frederick and G. Lowenstein, *Hedonic Adaptation in Well-being: The Foundations of Hedonic Psychology,* Ed. D. Kahneman, E. Diener, and N. Schwarz (New York: Russell Sage Foundation Press, 1999).
5. M.J. Fox, *Lucky Man* (New York: Hyperion, 2002).
6. Oregon Health Plan. The Prioritized List. www.oregon.gov/DHS/healthplan/priorlist/main.shtml

Rx 15

Professional Invalidism

When the patient needs the disease

Children at a very early age learn to manipulate their parents to get special attention and treats when they are ill. This may involve something as simple as being allowed to stay up later than usual after a day of flu symptoms or getting an extra day away from school by pretending to still be ill after the symptoms of a viral infection have resolved. Adults are equally prone to obtaining some extra attention and sympathy by exaggerating their symptoms or making a slow or incomplete recovery after an illness, operation, or injury. Perhaps if I tell my spouse that my incision is still really sore, I can get him to do some household chores that I really need to get done. These temptations are normal learned responses to illness but can become exaggerated to the point of becoming unhealthy–what psychiatrists refer to as "secondary gain" from an illness. It is a particular problem when the illness is prolonged, chronic, or, for children, due to inherited disease.

Hemophilia is perhaps one of the best examples of secondary gain in action. Although little has been written about the unique relationship of male hemophiliacs with their mothers, this is often, in my experience among hemophiliacs with associated liver disease, a very peculiar relationship that develops, at least in part because of the way the disease is inherited. The common form of this disease is inherited in what is called a sex-linked recessive pattern; only males are affected, and the recessive gene is inherited from the boy's mother and not from his father, who contributes a normal Y chromosome. The result is usually a marked tendency for the mothers to feel guilty about giving their sons a disease; and the sons, as they grow and develop progressive, sometimes disabling symptoms of the disease, can readily exploit that guilt for special attention from their mothers. The most famous example in history is that of Prince Alexei, the son of Tsar Nicholas II and his wife, Alexandra, of the Romanov Russian dynasty; he was a loser in the gene lottery because of the extensive intermarriage in the European royalty of the late nineteenth century, which led to the propagation of the hemophilia gene. Although the exact inheritance pattern of hemophilia was not appreciated at that time, the prince's hemophilia did lead to a clearly overly protective, guilt-driven pathological relationship with his mother. This was exploited by the lecherous monk Rasputin with disastrous consequences. Some historians believe that Prince Alexei's hemophilia and its effect on his mother ultimately contributed in a major way to the Russian revolution, the overthrow of the Tsar, and the end of the Romanov dynasty.

Hypochondriasis disorder, another recognized psychiatric illness, refers to an abnormal fear of having a serious illness and bears a superficial resemblance to the phenomenon of secondary gain but is really very different. Hypochondriacs do not have the disease that they worry excessively about and are generally physically healthy. Although hypochondriasis is a continuum and can include delusional beliefs about being ill, leading to secondary gain, most hypochondriacs are rational and can be reassured that they are not ill, although that may take a lot of extra testing and time on the part of their doctors. This may need to be repeated many times, as they frequently develop new fears of new diseases. This is perhaps best illustrated by the tendency of medical students to worry that they have the disease that they are currently studying. Hypochondriasis is probably also stimulated by the prevalent media attention to the hazards associated with normal daily living. One may find it difficult to avoid worrying about developing some serious disease when the daily headlines proclaim the dangers of WIFI in schools, cancers caused by chemicals leached out from our drinking and cooking utensils, and deadly bugs lurking on doorknobs, stethoscopes, or doctors' ties. The sound bites do not usually allow enough time to specify what the exact dangers are, or what cancers or infections they cause, thus sparing the worry promoters from the need to cite any scientific evidence. In this environment, we can all easily come to believe we are such fragile organisms that we must always be on high alert to the ever-present dangers all around us. But if that is the case, how did we manage to so overpopulate our planet? Even hypochondriacs do eventually die, and usually—as is true for many of us—of some serious illness; the fear of missing one of these diseases in a complaining hypochondriac leads to a lot of "rule out" diagnostic testing (see Chapter 13) by their doctors.

A third form of mental illness that is not recognized as such is, I believe, more common and dangerous than hypochondriasis. I refer to this as professional invalidism, and my tentative conclusion that this is a real disorder is based almost entirely on my own experiences, as I cannot find a good comprehensive description of it in the medical or psychiatric literature. Let me describe what I think are its characteristic features.

First, people with this disorder, unlike hypochondriacs, have a real disease, usually chronic but not life-threatening. They latch onto this disease as a possible explanation for all kinds of unrelated unpleasant symptoms or experiences and become focused on the disease to the exclusion of getting on with the rest of their lives. In short, they are unable to cope with being in less than perfect health. The disease is their entry point into the medical system, which they use to excess.

Second, the professional invalid's symptoms are multitudinous, entirely subjective, and bear no clear relationship to the disease that they know they have. The most common one is probably chronic fatigue (the symptom, not necessarily the disease), which is a common non-specific complaint of many healthy adults over the age of fifty. The symptoms of a professional invalid are by definition disabling and persistent, otherwise they could not consider themselves to be invalids. In these individuals, symptoms affect multiple body systems and lead them to abandon many activities of daily living and request help from homemakers, friends, and relatives just to get through the day. In this way, they may superficially share some characteristics of those who obtain secondary gain from being ill; in the professional invalid, however, the symptoms do not relate to any specific identifiable disease, although they all do have some chronic disease—this is their ticket into the medical marketplace.

Many times, the disabling symptoms start as soon as the chronic disease is diagnosed, a kind of labelling phenomenon, a well-recognized adverse effect of finding a disease. Most patients with high blood pressure, for example, do not have any symptoms related to it until they are aware of the problem, but there are serious negative consequences of that awareness, as evidenced by a decrease in the scores on a general health questionnaire in those labelled as having hypertension as compared to those who have it but are not aware of having it.[1] As another example of this labelling phenomenon, one study[2] found that patients labelled as having Lyme disease but who were later found to not have it, actually had more symptoms, made more visits to doctors and hospitals, and were more disabled than those who truly did have the disease. This report can be seen as a study of misdiagnoses or of the negative consequences of being labelled with a disease, whether or not you actually have it, depending on your viewpoint.

Third, professional invalids are notorious doctor shoppers and have many different specialists involved in their care, usually at least one for each major organ system. They will seldom tell the most recent doctor about the others until there is some discussion of the treatment, at which point the patient will mention that the doctors at some famous institution already tried that and it did not work. This doctor-shopping commonly results in the use of many different medications, often with serious side effects that may worsen one or more of the symptoms. In my experience, professional invalids become very attached to the need for multiple medications over long periods of time; if the doctors each prescribe several medications to try to relieve the ill-defined symptoms, the patient may soon be taking ten or more different medications daily and come to believe that they have to be taken forever. And these patients get psychological reinforcement that they must be seriously ill if they need all those pills just to stay alive. They tend naturally to become particularly attached to any narcotics they may be prescribed, even though in many cases the narcotics worsen symptoms such as nausea, constipation, and fatigue.

They are also susceptible to the suggestions of alternative medicine practitioners that what they really need is some natural or homeopathic concoction to correct the imbalance in their metabolism, and may be taking many natural remedies of dubious composition and safety. Some of my professional invalid patients insist that the only medication that has any effect on their symptoms is smoked marijuana. The oral pure tetrahydrocannabinol, which has the same effect on the brain as the smoked variety, is available as a prescription that I used frequently in my practice, but simply does not work for these individuals.

Doctor-shopping also inevitably leads to excessive investigation—it is easier to cut the tedious interview with a professional invalid short by agreeing to order a scan of some sort than it is to explain that no further investigations are indicated or necessary.

Last, and perhaps most characteristic of professional invalids, they enjoy stumping their doctors and are quite confident that no doctor will ever be able to make the right diagnosis and relieve their symptoms. In this they are almost always right. They look the doctor right in the eye and, while pleading for help, practically defy her to explain why they are ill. And if the doctor is so bold as to suggest that they try some simple remedy, they will have a ready explanation as to why it will not work. Often this explanation is that some other doctor has already tried that remedy and it did not work or even worsened the symptoms. It is not uncommon for the doctor of a professional invalid to go through a long series of suggestions and find that each has been tried unsuccessfully before, or that the patient claims to be allergic to the medication that is suggested.

When asked what they think is the cause of their symptoms, many professional invalids will suggest that they relate to some environmental sensitivity such as urea-formaldehyde foam insulation in their home, radon in the basement, or the negative effects on their health of the wind turbine that is visible on the distant horizon outside the living room window. However, even if they move to a new home without any of these hazards, the symptoms will persist, because in some perverse way, the professional invalid needs to have symptoms—symptoms become the entire focus of his life. We all know professional invalids from social situations in which an entire evening may be spent discussing their ill health if they are allowed to control the conversation. These are the individuals who will give you an organ-by-organ recital of their medical problems at the dinner table. In short, professional invalids enjoy poor health.

Of course, not every patient with multiple disabling and serious symptoms is a professional invalid; many unfortunate individuals are really seriously ill with symptoms related to multiple body systems, either because one disease has affected many parts, or because they have several different coexisting diseases that interact in complex ways. What distinguishes the professional invalid from such unfortunate people is their lack of objective evidence of serious disease, their tendency to describe all of their symptoms with superlatives, and the general refractoriness of any symptoms to any form of treatment. The patient with constant nausea due to diabetic effects on stomach motility (technically known as diabetic gastroparesis) will improve with one or other medications commonly used to stimulate stomach emptying; the professional invalid with constant nausea will not improve, or will find the side effects of the medication intolerable and stop taking it.

From the physician's perspective, trying to treat a professional invalid is a frustrating process. As with the hypochondriac, it is necessary to be as sure as possible that she does not have any serious organic basis for the symptoms, and this leads to excessive investigation that often reinforces the patient's conclusion that she must have some serious and mysterious disease—after all, why else would Doctor B order a repeat CT scan when Doctor A did one just three months ago and found nothing abnormal? These patients are prone to show up with a daily diary of symptoms that the doctor is expected to review for the critical clue to the problem and with a two-page list of questions that the doctor must answer in a scheduled fifteen-minute follow-up appointment.

My very perceptive staff developed an effective way of getting me out of such situations. When it was clear that I was stuck in the examining room with such a patient, my pager would call me out for an urgent phony phone call to allow me to cut short the frustrating process of trying to explain some symptoms that had no rational explanation. This may not have been the most honest way of dealing with such patients, but there really is no better one that I know of. (Incidentally, just because your doctor interrupts your next visit to take a phone call does not automatically mean that he considers you a professional invalid.) A more common way for doctors to cut this painful process short is to suddenly decide that they need some critical bit of lab work or some further imaging study and defer the discussion until that has been reported.

Is it possible that what I have described as professional invalidism is simply a rewording of an already described psychiatric disorder under a different name? It has been more than forty years since I did my training in psychiatry as an undergraduate medical student, and I am open to the possibility that this disorder is known in the world of psychiatry under a different label, but I cannot find anything that describes all of the characteristics. Professional invalids will typically vehemently deny that the symptoms could have a psychiatric basis, so it is possible that psychiatrists and psychologists rarely, if ever, see them because they will refuse to see a psychiatrist. "What! Do you think I'm crazy?" is likely to be the response to any suggestion that they should see any kind of mental health worker.

The symptoms certainly encompass some features of what psychiatrists call a passive-dependent personality disorder, or of one or more of the somatization disorders that include hypochondriasis. It differs from them in significant ways, however, most notably in the starting point of having a real chronic disease as the necessary trigger for the development of the disorder. Perhaps it is just secondary gain carried to an extreme degree. It may also have some features in common with a rather rare psychiatric disorder called Munchausen syndrome. Individuals with this disorder intentionally fake symptoms or even knowingly harm themselves to mimic a real disease and in the past have had surgery to remove a non-existent kidney stone or a normal appendix. They become very adept at mimicking real diseases and may, when no one is watching, hold the thermometer up to the light bulb to show that they have a fever, or contaminate a urine specimen to get an abnormal lab report. However, the person with Munchausen syndrome, unlike the professional invalid, is well aware of the real cause of the symptoms, as he has produced them. In contrast, the professional invalid truly believes that he is ill from some mysterious, unidentified disease—all those incompetent doctors just can't find out what it is.

Is professional invalidism a real disorder that is deserving of study, having a number attached to it (see Chapter 12), and being considered as a disease along with many other diseases that appear to have no organic basis? As I have described it, it is certainly not curable or even treatable in the usual sense, other than by patiently listening to the complaints and humbly admitting that you cannot explain them. But maybe that *is* the treatment. Dr. Lloyd Hession, a wise, long-gone professor of medicine in my days as a trainee in internal medicine, once commented that sometimes the worst thing a doctor can do for a patient is to cure her. The patient may then have nothing left to live for.

Notes

1. Gbenga Ogedegbe, "Labeling and Hypertension: It Is Time to Intervene on Its Negative Consequences," *Hypertension* 56 (2010): 344–45.

2. M.C. Reid, R.T. Schoen, J. Evans, J.C. Rosenberg, and R.I. Horowitz, "The Consequences of Overdiagnosis and Overtreatment of Lyme Disease: An Observational Study," *Annals of Internal Medicine* 128 (1998): 354–65.

Rx 16

Outside the Office

Thinking like a doctor

Many years ago, as a newly minted doctor, while strolling through an amusement park with my wife and daughter, I met a mother with an obviously disfigured and mentally challenged small child in a stroller. As we passed, the child let out a very unusual and distinctive scream. Without thinking, I immediately—and too loudly—commented to my wife, "*crie du chat* syndrome." I had never seen a patient with *crie du chat* (cry of the cat) syndrome, but had read and heard about it in my rotation in pediatrics during training. The startled but gracious mother heard me and turned to stare at me, then acknowledged that I was right about the diagnosis and guessed my profession correctly. We had a pleasant conversation about the difficulties of caring for a mentally challenged child. She informed me that this was not the first time some complete stranger had blurted out the diagnosis on hearing that cry, and that it had always been a doctor.

None of us can totally leave our work at the office, if that work involves the need for close and frequent observations of others. Malcolm Gladwell has written that a key to good writing is to get your mind to think like that of someone else, and uses a doctor as an example.[1] One of the difficulties of being a physician is that it becomes impossible, or at least very difficult, to not think like one. This includes observations made using all your senses even when you are off-duty and interacting with others, whether with good friends at the bridge table, golf course, or curling rink, or with casual acquaintances or even complete strangers on the street. Once you have been adequately trained and experienced as a physician, it is difficult to not make a diagnosis or at least suspect one when you see obvious signs of some disease state, even if the observation is made from across the room in a restaurant.

Although these observations are somewhat specialty specific, the signs are so obvious at times that the specialty does not matter—you desperately want to ask if the person is aware of their problem and is on appropriate treatment for the condition you have just diagnosed. What follows is a lighthearted and partial list of the specialty specific observations and thought processes that are likely to happen in doctors' casual out-of-the-office interactions.

The gynecologist is probably quicker than anyone else to observe the characteristic facial melasma of a young woman who is probably on an oral contraceptive or is pregnant.

The obstetrician will estimate the expected date of delivery on observing the bulging abdomen of a young woman and wonder if he might get the business on that date, although any comments about this can be very dangerous, as the bulge, even when very obvious, may not relate to pregnancy at all.

The pediatrician at the pool party will take note of the FLK (funny looking kid) and try to recall which gene defect on which chromosome is responsible for the Allagille syndrome she has just diagnosed.

The neurologist will, more quickly than most, note the slight tremor of early Parkinson's disease or try to mentally locate the exact location in the brain that has been affected by a stroke in someone with a partial paralysis of an arm or leg.

The family physician may well note the couple who seem to be avoiding each other and begin to wonder if there is an abuse problem or if they need some marital counselling.

Dermatologists may be most likely of all specialists to become absorbed in their medical observations, because their organ of interest, the skin, is most readily available for inspection—although palpation of the nodule revealed by the low-cut evening gown could get one into trouble quickly. Would that rash be best treated with a lotion or a cream? How can I persuade the deeply tanned gentleman in the corner that he should not get so much sun exposure? Is there a neglected melanoma hidden among all those solar keratoses on the beach-walker's back?

Even those whose specialty involves diseases of internal organs are unlikely to leave their work entirely in the office. Endocrinologists have a plethora of signs to note, including obvious eye signs that scream out the need for attention to thyroid problems. How can a doctor who has, on a casual encounter, made the instant diagnosis of an underactive thyroid gland, a very easily corrected problem, avoid the temptation to ask the stranger to have his thyroid checked?

The nephrologist is much more limited in making specialty specific observations, but will be quick to note the characteristic pasty pallor of someone with chronic kidney failure and will manoeuvre into position at the cocktail party to see if there is a dialysis fistula in the arm.

The respirologist will readily diagnose sleep apnea in the yawning Pickwickian in the restaurant booth at the truck stop, and probably will be very tempted to ask him why he is not using his CPAP machine to treat it. The respirologist and the cardiologist may come to different conclusions when they spot clubbing of the fingernails–is it due to congenital heart disease, cystic fibrosis, or lung cancer?

The anesthesiologist may muse about how difficult it would be to intubate the trachea of the fellow with obvious ankylosing spondylitis whose neck is so flexed that he can only stare at his own toes.

Surgeons are not immune to out-of-office preoccupations. The orthopedic surgeon will mentally analyze your abnormal gait and consider what kind of hip operation might benefit you. The plastic surgeon will no doubt assess how she could improve the appearance of the poorly healed scar on your neck, or imagine what your face would look like without the telltale fine facial wrinkles that betray a long history of smoking. General surgeons will be very critical of any exposed crooked surgical scar they observe, confident that they could have done a better job of stitching the wound back up. They may scratch their heads about exactly what operation was done when a bikini-exposed surgical scar pops into view. Of all abdominal scars, perhaps those due to past liver transplantation are the most dramatic and puzzling to non-physicians, but it will often be immediately obvious to an experienced surgeon. These "Chevron" or "Mercedes" scars are also more likely than most to be deliberately exposed, as most organ recipients are keen to be identified as such, and willing to discuss with complete strangers the need for more organ donors.

The pathologist may well lapse into musing about what he might find if he gets the job of doing the autopsy on the cadaveric fellow in the corner of the bar.

What is the psychiatrist most likely to observe in casual social encounters? There was a time when a retired psychiatrist played in a bridge group with us. He seemed perfectly normal both mentally and physically to me, as did the other couples we played with. However, at one point, after another couple had left, he commented to me about the schizoid personality disorder of the gentleman who had just left. This left me wondering what kind of psychiatric diagnosis he had made on me. The psychiatrist in social settings can usually be counted on to come up with some complicated, long name for the condition that the rest of us would label as simply being a bore or being an egocentric s.o.b.

In my own field of liver disease, there are abundant opportunities and temptations to extend the make-a-diagnosis game outside the office, and at times it is almost impossible to not do so. On a few social occasions, I have detected the very dramatic and characteristic odour of fetor hepaticus (similar to that of a natural gas leak) and tried to figure out who in the room had chronic liver disease and was exhaling this odour, unwilling to consider the more dangerous possibility that there actually was a gas leak in the building. It is easy to speculate about whether the spider nevi on the face of the woman across the room is due to pregnancy, alcoholic liver disease, or one of the more interesting chronic liver diseases that I treated. Is that just a beer belly, or is there free fluid that should be drained off that protuberant abdomen? Hepatologists are also prone to keeping track of the number of drinks consumed by the fellow who has stayed close to the bar all evening; and wondering if he is one of the unlucky heavy drinkers who will eventually need their services.

In many ways, these observations are no different for the medical professional than for anyone else whose livelihood depends on regular and perceptive observations of others. The dentist will be observing your teeth and figuring out what could be done to improve them as you talk to him at the dinner party. The optometrist will be mentally analyzing your eyeglass prescription when you are trying to impress her with your brilliant conversation and may be wondering how to direct the conversation to your need for contact lenses, or a better-fitting frame. The banker or accountant will steer the conversation to your investment portfolio if you give the impression that you may have enough money to need an investment adviser. The hairdresser will be the first to notice the differently coloured roots, and the barber the first to note, but hopefully keep quiet about, the irregular neck hair line shave. The clergyman is most likely to first take note of the cross on your necklace before starting a conversation with you. The bored dietitian at the cocktail party will be mentally estimating the body mass index of everyone present, while the off-duty journalist will be eavesdropping on conversations, looking for a newsworthy story, perhaps about a victim confessing to have fallen for some financial scam. And the scammer on the opposite side of the room will be eavesdropping on the fellow talking to the accountant, to pick out his next target.

Even in non-social settings, the temptation to make assumptions about the people you encounter may be pervasive. The pharmacist watching you looking for the right dye for your graying hair may conclude that you have been taking a drug called amiodarone too long if she notices your very bluish, discoloured nose and will somehow persuade you to discuss your heart problems. The tailor or dressmaker no doubt is a keen observer of the attire of both casual acquaintances and strangers on the street, and may wonder who let the guy with the style that is so yesterday out the door looking like that. The vacationing police officer no doubt cannot escape checking the exposed tattoos on the beach for the telltale characteristics of a biker gang membership or a stay in the Big House as a guest of Her Majesty. The funeral director at our fishing camp has probably, on a slow morning on the river, mused about how much work he would have to make this aging countenance look realistic at an open-coffin visitation, although that will not happen if I get my wish for cremation.

There is no cure for this phenomenon, and really no need for a cure, but there is a definite need to be aware of it and to develop self-restraint to keep it in check. The jeweller should refrain from commenting on the fake diamonds. The used-car salesman should resist the temptation to try his sales pitch on the others at the barbeque party. And the list goes on and on. We all do it and need to be aware of it and consider how these subliminal assessments may be interfering with our interactions outside the office.

At times, I have deliberately tried to think like some other professional, to avoid the temptation to make first-impression diagnoses on strangers or casual acquaintances. I have tried to deliberately think as a tailor might, and observe clothing styles closely to get some nonmedical impression of the people I meet. But I do not have the mental equipment or knowledge to do so. I cannot tell an Armani suit from a cheap imitation; as many of my colleagues know, my fashion sense is nonexistent. My co-workers have marvelled at my uncanny ability to pick clashing colour schemes and style combinations when I manage to get out the door before the wardrobe committee (my wife) has had a chance to check me out. My efforts to think like other professionals are no more successful; even trying to think like another specialist in a different branch of medicine is sometimes difficult—I can't even tell the difference in the gait of someone with hip arthritis from that of someone with a bad knee.

Are mechanics, architects, engineers, computer geeks, and factory workers less prone to analyzing and developing first impressions of the people they meet based on their work experience than are professionals who work with people daily? After all, they work largely with inanimate objects rather than with people. I will never be able to find out, because I just can't think like them. I can't stop thinking like a doctor. My brain wiring has been permanently altered by my years of medical training and experience. Perhaps some social scientist can devise the experiment to see if there is a systematic difference in social interactions based on the type of job you do. But I suspect there is—computer whizzes are not called "geeks" for no reason, and the bike mechanic is not called a "wrench" because of his social skills.

Notes

1. M. Gladwell, *What the Dog Saw* (New York: Little, Brown and Company, 2009).

About the Author

Dr. Ghent was born and raised in the rural community of Mount Forest, Ontario, Canada. After elementary education in a one-room rural schoolhouse, he attended Mount Forest District High School. Following two years of general science at the University of Western Ontario, he was accepted into the medical school there, graduating in 1970. Four years of training in internal medicine and gastroenterology in London followed and then three years in training and research in liver diseases at Yale University School of Medicine in New Haven, Connecticut. Returning to join the Faculty of Medicine at the University of Western Ontario in 1977, he became a leading member of the liver transplant team at its inception in the early 1980s and remained affiliated with the teaching hospital and the transplant program until he retired in 2011. He was awarded the Distinguished Clinician award of the Department of Medicine in 2007 and the Distinguished Service Award by the Canadian Association for the Study of the Liver in 2011. He lives in London with his wife, Vera Simon. In retirement, he enjoys bicycling, duplicate bridge, curling, fly fishing, fly tying (and writing).

This is the first book he has written for the general public, although he has authored more than 100 scientific papers, book chapters, reviews, editorials, and other scholarly works for the scientific community.